Training on Empty
Lize Brittin

Dedicated to my mother, Janine Brittin.

* * *

Thank you for respecting the author's work.

* * *

TABLE OF CONTENTS

* * *

Foreword

Athletic competition is a heroic journey. The late scholar Joseph Campbell, himself an athlete, brilliantly describes the path of the hero in his book, Hero of a Thousand Faces. The seeker, in the quest for the fulfillment of a dream, ventures into the unknown. Whether the prize sought is as lofty as an Olympic gold medal or as modest as completing one's first 5k race it becomes in itself the representation of something of greater inherent value – the process of personal transformation that springs from accepting and loving a part of self that previously remained in shadow. The excitement to go into new territory soon leads one face to face with the limitations of the status quo – once committed the onus is on the seeker to remake her/himself or collapse into the hell of an unrealized life.

Recently I was a guest speaker at a Women's Quest Retreat, run by my colleague and lifelong friend Colleen Cannon. The women that come to these week-long fitness adventures are typically successful middle-class, self-aware, body-conscious, mothers, sisters and daughters. This evening I thought to ask how many of them liked their bodies. I expected at least half. I was shocked when of the 28 participants only 2 raised their hands. Interestingly enough those two hands did not rise from the young, sleek beauties, but from two of the senior women who had taken the heroic journey, perhaps many times. On the subject of their earthly vehicle they had finally come to rest at a point of appreciation. The other women all wished for a physical composition other than the one they possessed.

The human body, male or female is an astonishing piece of machinery, which we are told is made in the image of the Creator. You just can't get much better than that. So what is this mantle of depreciation and deprecation that the majority of modern women don that makes them feel self-hatred at their own image?

If we go way back we can see that ever since Eve got blacklisted for giving Adam an apple, women have had a hard time getting their rightful esteem throughout history. Coupling with this undervaluation of the feminine is an overvaluation of the male attribute of aggression through the sustained misappropriation of youthful testosterone into acts of war. The masculine/feminine relationship remains polarized to this day, massively leaking the ingredients of potential miracles.

While the see-saw of gender roles and responsibilities greatly shifted in the 20th century this polarity remains. The car and TV as household items have ushered in the nuclear family for western civilization and we have hailed the pill as the liberation of women and the breakdown of sexual stereotypes. But there has been a trade-off. When women made the inroads into the affairs of men the status of her biologically-mandated role as nurturer took a hit. Institutions took over the role of grandmothers, moved birth out of the hands of midwives into the surgical units of hospitals, and separated babies from their mothers after delivery. The symbol of Mother, the breast, was deemed inferior to the bottle; human milk inferior to a cow's. In the 70's economics shunted women out of the home into the workforce en masse, and children into daycares. The family garden plot went to high-rise condos and the source of food became a supermarket. Home-made soup alchemized with mother's loving hands has now been supplanted with a plethora of pseudo-foods imbued with cold steel and a profit margin behind them. Consequently most western societies suffer from a deficiency of the most basic building block of physical and emotional development that sets us up for health, happiness and the fulfillment of our potential – Mothering. We have been duped, and earthlings are in real trouble because of it.

Our fundament, Mother Earth, has slid to the bottom of totem pole. Her denunciation is a meme personalized through the bodies of women – a miserable slab of granite formed over eons, to which both genders are shackled. Anorexia, bulimia, fatness and thinness, the shrouding and mutilation of women, addiction to superficial forms of beauty, and myriad ways in which women are debased, belong to us all. Sadly this issue has been largely cloaked with secrecy, and inadequately confined to the realm of the individual, rather than addressed collectively. All this brings me to a time where I encounter 26 out of 28 fit, healthy, modern women who are deeply ashamed of their bodies. Among them and behind them is a silent epidemic of girls and women living in a land of unprecedented material supplies who do not even feel entitled to the essential right to feed themselves adequately.

The exploration of the athletic potential of the female body has and will continue to be a face-off with this dense paradigm. Invariably it is one of those obstacles encountered by any woman who undertakes the heroic journey in an athletic arena, as Lize Brittan did. A brilliant young athlete full of hope for a top career, Lize hit the rock at full speed. It almost killed her. Lize's story is both heart-rending and inspiring. But more importantly her journey of self-discovery so candidly delivered and interspersed with practical and meaningful guidance, offers a unique road-map of the eating-disorder territory, especially for athletic women. The dilemma of the act of running as both savior and executioner is harrowing to read, as are her flirtations with death in an excruciating slow suicide attempt by starvation. But even in despair Lize's spark shines through with courage and intelligence. Her eventual apotheosis of learning to surrender to the feminine deserves nothing short of a standing ovation.

With this fascinating and informative memoir a big chunk of granite has been broken off, a women's soul restored to life, and a call to others to take the heroic journey resounds. As a society the job is not done until the last piece of the monolith has been chipped away and transmuted into a new paradigm where the magnificence of our physicality, male and female, is freely nurtured and expressed without apology.

Lorraine Moller
Olympic Marathon Bronze medalist
Author of *On the Wings of Mercury*

* * *

Introduction

Despite my intensely reckless and very unhealthy behavior, I am still alive. At my lowest point, I weighed less than 80 pounds at a height of five feet four inches. I was having seizures and was in the beginning stages of complete organ failure. I was jaundiced. My pituitary gland wasn't functioning properly. My hair was falling out, and my skin was scaly. I had edema and was constantly thirsty. I looked like a concentration camp victim, yet I felt fat all the time. I had lost touch with reality. I was anorexic.

Anorexia is – pardon the expression – a heavy topic. For more than one reason, it's not the kind of thing to bring up at the dinner table. Then again, how many anorexics actually sit down to eat dinner? It's a sad, painful, scary and destructive path that an anorexic takes-a path that the people around her often end up being forced to travel as well.

I became anorexic when I was 13. It happened in what seemed like an instant. I made a firm decision that I was going to lose weight, and there was no turning back. It wasn't so terrible at first. I even got more popular as the pounds dropped away. Eventually though, things got weird – really weird. For nearly 20 years after that initial decision, I battled the disease. My attitude toward life took a serious turn, and I let anorexia and all its deception take its all-consuming course.

It wasn't until much later, well after I had turned onto the road of recovery, that I realized what had been missing from that dark time in my life: humor. After that revelation, I decided to take a different look at this whole anorexia situation, and while I am in no way aiming to make light of the severity of anorexia and its consequences – according to The Alliance for Eating Disorders Awareness, 20 percent of people suffering from anorexia die prematurely from complications related to the disease – I do want to point out that humor heals. For me, it was a big part of getting well. Laughing again after so many years of being silent was an outlet, a way to save myself from the despair of an illness that almost killed me.

I don't mean to imply that this book is a comedy. I think George Carlin was probably one of the few brave enough to take on anorexia as a comedic topic. What I mean to say is that once I was able to smile again, I realized how dark my life had been while struggling with the illness. When I could fully laugh again, I knew I was on my way to recovery and out of the turmoil that had engulfed me for so long.

My name is Lize. This is the story of my life. This book is meant to give people an idea of what led to my anorexia, how I survived and how I began to heal. Unfortunately, there is no grand formula for getting well, no 12 steps or going cold turkey. However, I do believe there is a way out of the darkness. Each person must create his or her own path to recovery, but perhaps reading what I went through will offer some hope, inspiration and ideas to help others create a path to wellness. I tend to not do things half-assed, so taking anorexia to the extreme was almost predictable. As bad off as I was, however, I found a way. And if I recovered, there's hope for many others.

* * *

PART I – Red

Chapter 1: My So-Called Life

"An illness is like a journey into a far country; it sifts all one's experience and removes it to a point so remote that it appears like a vision." -Sholem Asch

On an exceptionally cold February night in 1997, after a series of seizures, I was rushed to the hospital with chest pain and shortness of breath. At the age of 30, I weighed 80 pounds. I wasn't expected to make it through the night. However, to everyone's surprise and amazement, including my own, I pulled through. It was obvious that I needed help, but since none of the nearby eating-disorder treatment facilities had any openings, I was moved to the hospital's cancer unit for three days in order to stabilize. I found it disturbingly ironic that I was surrounded by people fighting for their lives, while I was slowly killing myself.

Starvation is considered one of the most slow and painful ways to die. The body can last a long time without food. Typically, people who starve themselves don't die from an actual lack of food, but from related complications. As the body starts eating itself to keep the brain functioning, muscles and organs begin to atrophy. Organ failure or a heart attack is a common end for anorexics.

The entire time I was in the hospital, I was prodded, probed and tested. I was hooked to an intravenous saline drip in order to regulate my electrolytes. I slept in short shifts, a few hours at a time throughout both the days and nights, taking Tylenol for the excruciating headaches that manifested as my body fought for equilibrium. I ate even less than I had been eating before hospitalization, and I was exhausted from all the blood draws and tests being performed. The longer the lab-rat routine continued, the weaker I became. At one point, a nurse led me to a shower where, after just a few minutes standing on my own, my legs started to quiver beneath me. Once the fastest high-school athlete in all of Colorado, there I was, unable to even stand on my own two feet. I sat down on the shower's built-in bench and cried as the water splashed over my skin.

After the third day of tests, the doctors told me they wanted to keep me in the hospital a few more days to run even more tests. I was no expert, but the problem seemed pretty obvious to me: My body was malnourished and completely depleted. In short, I was too thin. More tests, it seemed to me, were not going to reveal anything more about my condition, so I threw a minor tantrum and was released. Sleep-deprived, emotionally spent and bruised from all the IV's and other needling, I headed home. The freedom of merely being outside in the fresh air after three solid days of being stuck in the hospital was overwhelming.

There are people whose lives are complicated by some kind of addiction all around. Many of these people are in denial or accept their addiction as part of who they are, often adhering to the adage, "once an alcoholic, always an alcoholic." There are others who live with the agony of knowingly operating below their true potential, yet are unable to change. They are intelligent and honest, open about their self-inflicted enslavement, yet completely frustrated by their inability to stop their self-sabotaging behavior. However, there are a lucky few who see beyond their addiction, finding both the courage and the astounding strength to break free from their addictions and jump full force into the unknown territory of recovery.

Heidi is one of these lucky few. I met her shortly before I wound up in the hospital. Over time, she became my mentor and my friend, my counselor and my inspiration. Radiant and strong, Heidi is the kind of person who lights up the room when she enters, a goddess if there ever was one. Her compassion and wisdom go far beyond the realm of what is considered normal in this world. I was immediately drawn to her.

When she was young, Heidi was bulimic. Over time, she forced herself to throw up so much that the acid from her stomach began to irritate her esophagus. At one point, she vomited so much blood that she nearly died right there on her bathroom floor. As she lay with her head on the floor, half passed out, Heidi decided she didn't want to die, that there had to be a way out. And just like that, she stopped binging and purging. It's almost unheard of to have the bravery and the will to do something like that, but Heidi had an idea that a brilliant destiny and a better life were awaiting her. She became one of the few women I know who fully beat an eating disorder. I know a lot of women in various stages of recovery; a few have found a way out. Heidi is one of these few.

It takes a magnanimous human being to see the potential behind the illness in a person. Without Heidi, I would have been lost. Her guidance and love helped me find my own path out of addiction and away from the trappings of anorexia. It was a long time before I got even a little bit better, but Heidi helped open my mind to the possibility of getting well, and that was a necessary first step. Once released from the hospital, I started meditating and reading books on spirituality, something that had been missing from my life for years. I opened up my mind, exploring auras and the occult, and I became fascinated with energy and the correlation between intention and manifestation. As a runner, I felt it was necessary to picture myself running well in a race the night before and anticipate that what

I imagined could become a reality. The idea was that events would unfold as I imagined they would. Facing a challenge of a different sort, I began to understand how the power of positive thinking could be applied to other areas of my life. Unfortunately, while these new revelations were of great benefit to my soul, I hoped, they did little to improve or correct my self-destructive patterns, and I was still restricting my caloric intake and exercising for incredibly long periods of time each day.

Before I became anorexic, I was at least a somewhat well-rounded child and engaged with the world. I painted and drew, cooked, read books and watched movies. By contrast, my life became very limited and myopic once I became anorexic. I don't recall doing much of anything once my weight became so abnormally low. I also don't recall exactly when it was that I effectively stopped being in the world. I was isolated, except for a few select friends who could tolerate the sight of me, and I had dropped all hobbies and interests from my life. Many anorexics are utterly lost in their illness; they no longer have a sense of who they are, what they like or what ignites passion in their hearts. Even at a devastatingly low weight, I spent days on end exercising even though I lacked any real strength. Looking back, I don't know how I managed.

I also spent my time anticipating the two small meals I allowed myself every day – one in the evening, one late at night. With hunger, time seems to pass more slowly, and because I would allow myself to eat only at certain times, so much time was wasted waiting. I was too hungry to throw myself into a book or engage in anything that required too much thought or energy, so I waited, watching the clock but trying not to be too obvious about it. Occasionally, there were days on which I would eat more normally and even some days on which I would binge, but the guilt was extreme and often very hard to handle. At the time, I couldn't see that those days on which I ate normally were what my body, mind and spirit craved. At what point in my life had I had lost balance?

Anorexia, for me, was somewhat of a "frog-being-boiled-in-a-pot" situation, a slow evolution in which I subconsciously managed to ignore the water heating up around me. For those not familiar with the term, it is in reference to a study done in which two frogs are placed in different pots of water. In one pot, the water is boiling. Naturally, the frog jumps out in an instant. The frog in the other pot, on the other hand, is put in warm water first, and the water is gradually heated to a boil. In this case, the frog will stay put until it is boiled alive. With any addiction there typically comes a point at which the addicted person becomes aware of how bad things have become. This is the point where she might ask, "How did I get here?" or "How did it get this bad?" The answer, of course, is that these things don't happen overnight. Getting to a low point – or as addicts put it, "hitting rock bottom" – takes time. It's by taking many small steps toward insanity that the sane become insane, just in the same way it takes many small steps by the guru to achieve enlightenment. I didn't just wake up one day with a full-blown eating disorder, it became part of my life so gradually I didn't realize it was happening. My desire and determination to change happened in an instant, but the disorder took hold slowly. Over time the illness took over, and I realized somewhere along the way that I was stuck. It was too late to do anything, so I stayed the destructive course until eventually my body forced me to stop. Despite never quite having a sense of what was normal growing up, I didn't cross the line into severe illness until I was a teen. Still, my childhood was far from perfect.

* * *

Chapter 2 – Welcome to the Real World

"Being born is like being kidnapped. And then sold into slavery." – William Shakespeare

I was born too soon. The doctors had set a random date for my mom's Cesarean section, even though I had given no sign that I was ready to enter this world. I must have been quite content floating around in my mom's womb, surrounded by warmth and getting nourishment as needed. Who the hell wants to leave that for the cold operating room? But on January 21, 1967, at 8 a.m., I was abruptly pulled out, slapped, and introduced to what must have been my first sense of the unfairness of the world.

I grew up in a fairly typical household. Despite people often thinking that the youngest child in the family gets all the perks, I'm not convinced. Being the youngest in the family had its disadvantages. I was subjected to relentless bullying from my older sister, and I had two older half-brothers who also knew how to tease. My much older half-sister from my dad's side, whom I rarely saw, stayed out of the fray. The result of all this pestering from others was the gradual grinding down of my self-esteem. By the time I was four, I decided I wanted to kill myself. Now, how a four-year-old gets an idea so severe is one of those unexplained mysteries we may never solve, but that was my plan.

I discussed this idea with my fully functioning, alcoholic father, who asked how I would accomplish such a goal. Being a scientist, he was all about method. In asking my father, who was not psychologically inclined, I was seeking a compassionate response that might make me feel better. I told him that I thought jumping off a cliff would work. I wasn't sure where to find cliffs, but I was sure they existed somewhere, because I had seen them on TV. Instead of offering sympathy and some comfort, my dad merely let me know that I would get hurt if I embarked on such a leap. Well, that was no good! I was trying to get out of the pain that I had endured in my four short years on earth. Hum, well, I rationalized; I would use a ladder then. Of course this resolved the going-to-hurt issue, but completely ruined both the actual jumping part and also the much needed "splat" at the end that causes death, my ultimate goal, to occur. When I related this to my dad, he just laughed.

I don't recall any further discussion on the topic, which today strikes me as odd. I think things were different back then, and children weren't encouraged to talk about feelings or fears. Being the youngest in a very vocal family often left me unheard anyway, and I think I was in grade school before I actually finished an entire sentence. I grew up speaking half-sentences, because my relatives were too impatient to wait for me to finish. My siblings and parents were loud, smart, talkative and impatient. I, on the other hand, was contemplative, reserved and often dreaming of other, better places. I ultimately concluded that the best solution was to just swallow or push aside any feelings or fears and move on with what I felt was my sad, insignificant life.

Although I eventually managed to hold my own, the effects of those early days persisted. Even now, if I'm under stress, I stammer and hesitate when I speak.

By the time I was six, I was overweight. Looking back at old pictures, I would say that I was chubby, if that. Everyone else called me fat, though. This surprises me, because the way I was teased, one would expect to see an obese person in those old pictures, not someone who could almost pass for normal. It's possible that I was using food to help squelch all of those uncomfortable feelings, but in any event, I never felt full. I was always fixated on food, and I didn't understand the art of living, apart from that of eating. Everything I did related to food. When planning to go swimming with a group of kids, I was focused on exactly what candy bar I would buy after we got out of the pool. If one of the parents in the neighborhood took a group of us shopping, the candy section was the first part of the store to catch my eye, and I always made sure to save some cash to buy a little something to munch on during the car ride home. Spoiling dinner never seemed to be a problem, because no matter how much candy I ate before dinner, there seemed to be enough room in my stomach for a full meal when my mother, a native of France, called us to the table with a shout of "a table!", French for "come to the table."

Despite our occasional fights, my sister and I liked to spend time together. We had separate rooms, but on occasion I would drag my mattress off my bed and into her room for a mini-slumber party. I would bring my stuffed Snoopy dog, my pillow and a snack that I had hidden in my pillowcase. My snack was usually a package of large Sweet Tarts – two oversized servings of the hard, not chewy, version of the treat; one cherry and one grape, each approximately three inches in diameter and wrapped in cellophane. My sister and I would talk until late into the night. When I was convinced that she had fallen asleep, I would reach into my pillowcase and pull out the Sweet Tart. It seemed that no matter how quietly I tried to unwrap it, I always woke my sister, who would ask what the noise was. "Nothing," I would reply, hoping she believed me, but she knew I was eating snacks I wasn't supposed to have. On those nights, she would never rat me out. Instead, she would ask for a bite. Satisfied, she would turn back over and fall asleep again, leaving me to finish my forbidden candy in peace. She never seemed obsessed with food like I was.

In kindergarten, I was the kid who was always picked last, or if lucky, second to last. I was last in races, too. Others saw me as completely nonathletic, even though I walked about mile to school and back almost every day. It's not that I didn't enjoy sports. On the contrary, I loved kickball and swimming and playing on the playground. I just hated playing with the other kids who were quick to criticize my slow pace or lack of coordination. Although I didn't always succeed, even at a young age I was putting pressure on myself to try to perform or look good in front of others.

Some will say that the youngest child in a family gets coddled and spoiled. I would say that it's not all it's cracked up to be. Not only was I the youngest in my family, I was also the youngest in the neighborhood. Being the "baby" of the group naturally set me apart from the others. I didn't have many real friends and became a loner very early in my childhood. I did have one friend in the neighborhood who was a year older than I was. Our being younger allowed us to form a bond, but because she was still slightly older, we were in different classes in school. It was a treat for me to be able to play with her as time and our schedules permitted, and spending time with her led to what I consider some of my best childhood memories.

In addition to being constantly criticized for having a chubby body, I was also teased simply for being my age. Occasionally the others would allow me to participate in their activities, but I had to endure their demanding orders and cruel comments– not a fair or pleasant compromise. Most of the time I was forced to sit on the sidelines and watch, hoping that I'd one day be old enough to join in all the fun and games.

I didn't learn until I was in my mid-twenties that during this period in my life, some much older kids in the neighborhood had tried to force me to be their "porn star" by demanding that I pose in provocative positions and expose myself while they took pictures. Even today I have no recollection of the incident, except of the dress I wore that day. It was one that my mom had made for me. She said I had worn it that day. Apparently I was forced to lift it up for the camera. When my mom saw the pictures, which I never saw, she broke down in sobs. She told me that I looked vacant and she could tell I had been coerced into doing it. How could I repress something I assume was so extremely traumatic? I'm not sure, but this all this came out during my second hospitalization for anorexia. However, once again, nobody ever talked to me about the incident at the time.

While I still have no recollection of the event, I have discovered that as upset as my mom was at the time, she didn't know how to approach the topic with me. Having grown up in a severely abusive environment as a child, her main focus was how to simply survive, not how to effectively communicate. When I was growing up, most parents didn't openly discuss feelings, emotions or problems in the household. In the case of my home life, better methods of communication were not encouraged until later.

This wasn't the last time I would be taken advantage of. I believe that these incidents contributed to my increasing sense of powerlessness, and ultimately led me to try to regain power through other means. My sense of helplessness was increased by the fact that my dad was a binge-drinking alcoholic. Life with someone who drinks is miserable no matter how you slice it, and my life was no exception. I witnessed him harass my oldest brother, make a fool of himself in public, and torment the entire family with his verbal abuse. The contrast between his professional life as a well-respected theoretical physicist and the mess he was at home was tremendous. It's hard to believe that he served as the chairman of the physics department at the University of Colorado given his drive to drink.

When I was twelve, my father kicked me out in a

drunken rampage. I could hear him yelling at me that I was stupid and retarded as I ran for my neighbor's house. Even though he didn't physically abuse me, the threat of it was always there. The threat of verbal and emotional abuse was a given. He scared me, and at times I hated him with every fiber of my being. My siblings and I never knew what to expect when it came to my dad's behavior. We used to have to call home and ask our mother if it was "safe" or "clear" to bring a friend home. "Is Dada drunk?" was the question we continually posed. My sister began keeping a diary when she was eight, and it is filled with page after page starting with, "Dear Diary, Dada is drunk." Rare were the days that we had any respite from his unpredictable behavior. I sometimes wonder if I would have felt more loved by my dad if he hadn't been drinking. It's hard to say, because I never got to know him away from his addiction. I also didn't know that many years later, I would recreate this pattern of chaos in the partners I chose. Sometimes what is familiar is more enticing than what feels good. I'm convinced that the love I had for my dad wouldn't have been buried under so much anger and disappointment had he been sober more often.

* * *

"We worry about what a child will become tomorrow, yet we forget that he is someone today." – Stacia Tauscher

My dad wanted a boy. In the 1960's, it wasn't common for fathers to be a part of the birth of a child. Instead, the doctors would later inform the new dad in the waiting room or at home, "Congratulations, it's a boy," or "You have yourself a healthy girl." My father had accepted the latter news twice already. A child with his first wife was a girl, and his first child with his second wife, my mom, was also a girl. My two half-brothers were from my mother's previous marriage. All my father's hopes for his own male offspring rested on my unborn shoulders. There was no way to alter the DNA that was already in place, so with his full disappointment, I came into being.

Growing up, I considered myself a tomboy. I wasn't a typical tomboy, though – the kind who is skinny with wild hair, wears jeans, climbs trees and plays in the mud. Instead, I was just anti-anything frilly and rejected anything girlish. In sharp contrast to my sister's clean, well-kept stuffed animal collection, my animals were losing stuffing, dirty and missing ears and whiskers. I played with dump trucks and hated dresses, but I was also quite afraid of adventure. In fact, trees were just not something I considered climbing, and even non-threatening playground equipment, such as the geo-dome climbing structure on the school grounds, often worried me. However, I still tried to be boy-like. One year I cut my hair short and wore a t-shirt to school every single day, even on picture day. I never felt pretty, especially compared to my sister, who was rail-thin with beautiful straight hair down to her waist. I feel today that since I felt I was lacking in the looks category, I was trying to get some kind of approval from my dad by being as much like a boy as I could.

During these early years, while I was trying to survive grade school, I developed a growing hatred of my body. It seemed entirely impossible for me to control the fat that was accumulating around my middle and thighs. I didn't correlate all the extra snacks with being fat. I thought I was just built that way, and I hated it. I even beat my stomach with my fists and cut other parts of my body with an X-ACTO-knife on occasion, turning all my anger at the world onto myself. Scratching bloody lines on my arm seemed to relieve some of the self loathing, but there was no escaping it entirely. Still, books like *The Ugly Duckling*, in which an ugly little bird grows into a beautiful swan, gave me a hint of hope that maybe one day things would change. I didn't know how or when, but I kept hoping that one day I would "show" all those bullies in my life. I hoped, too, that they would be sorry for calling me names, teasing me and ignoring me. Little did I know that I would eventually choose the ultimate form of cutting off my nose to spite my face.

In terms of physical maturation, everyone around me seemed to be a late bloomer. I, on the other hand, developed early. The day I got my period I remember thinking, "Oh no, this can't be happening, not yet!" I had just turned 12. I changed my underwear when I got home without telling anyone and went to bed hoping it was all a big mistake, that it would just go away. Unfortunately, the next morning the blood had soaked through my recently changed underwear and onto the sheets. Eight days and far too many maxi pads later, my mom dragged me to the gynecologist. Apparently I had a bit of a hormone imbalance. I was reassured that with time, everything would even out, and my periods wouldn't be so long and bloody. It was two months before my next spotty period, and after that I developed amenorrhea due to starving myself. Once I became anorexic I wouldn't have another menstrual period for 20 years.

Shortly after I started my adolescent journey, while I was wrestling my way through 5th grade, I picked up horseback riding. I'm not sure what caused me to want to start riding, but one day I got tired of sitting around so much. I wanted to do something different that I could claim as my own. Everyone in the neighborhood was athletic and thin; we had five cheerleaders on one block. I had tried dance, swimming, hiking, basketball and even gymnastics, and while I did an okay job in all of these sports, none really resonated with me. Besides, swim suits, leotards and shorts did not exactly make my plump body look glamorous. My parents allowed me to take a few riding lessons and after just one, I knew this was the sport for me. I loved it. It made me feel free, and for once in my life, I wasn't the fattest girl in the group! One of the girls in my weekly lessons was a good 15 pounds heavier than I was. I began riding Western, but the minute I saw one of the advanced riders jumping, I wanted to switch to English. Western riding and English riding differ not only in the equipment used, but in the events offered. English riding, with its smaller saddle and less restrictive style, appealed to me. I liked the idea of the horse and rider having more freedom to move. Soon I was entering shows and even winning ribbons. My sister began riding as well, and the two of us begged our parents for a horse.

Horseback riding isn't exactly the safest sport in the world. There were times when I was bucked, reared or thrown off, stepped on and even bitten. Twice my horse fell with me. At various times, I was thrown on top of the wooden post that holds the fence, was hit in the head when my horse threw his head back, and blacked out when I hit the ground after being bucked off a runaway horse. Despite the danger, riding was more often fun than not, and I refused to give it up no matter how much my mom worried. For me, riding was not only a sport; it was a way to be social. In addition, I felt that riding allowed me to experience some newly found confidence.

One day while I was having trouble focusing on

my schoolwork, I overheard a girl talking about riding. After class, I approached her and asked if she owned a horse. She said that she took lessons at a nearby barn, but didn't own a horse yet. We talked about riding and our riding instructors and eventually became good friends. Although we rode at different barns, I would occasionally visit her at her barn to watch her ride. Both of us desperately wanted to own a horse. She was a better rider than I was and had been riding since she was a little girl. I envied not only her elegant riding style but also her slim body. She and the horse she rode looked beautiful together.

Eventually, after so much begging, my parents decided to buy my sister and me a horse. Owning a horse meant that we spent a great deal of time at the barn where we kept Michelob, our palomino quarter-horse. In the summer, my sister and I would spend the mornings riding and taking lessons. Then our instructor would take the two of us, along with a few other girls who rode at the barn, to Taco Bell for lunch. Our favorite meal consisted of a Burrito Supreme with extra cheese and sour cream loaded with the contents of several hot-sauce packets. This was followed by a Coke or Pepsi to wash it all down. Occasionally, we would head to Wendy's for burgers, fries and a chocolate Frosty instead. After lunch, we would return to the barn to help with chores such as cleaning out stalls or mucking out the runs, and then go for a dip in the creek or go inner tubing down the ditch that was connected to the creek. I always felt melancholy returning home in the evening after a long day at the barn. These were some of the best summer days a young girl could imagine.

About a year after my sister and I got Michelob, we followed our instructor to a new, larger barn. I entered junior high school shortly after our horse was settled in his new surroundings. Oddly enough, the kids in junior high were not as mean to me as some of the kids in grade school had been. I had a few more friends there, and at the barn, I eventually met Amber, a girl in high school who seemed quite okay hanging out with me even though I was a few years younger. Amber was cool. She smoked Marlboro Lights, drank beer, and went to parties and concerts. I smoked my first cigarette with her, drank my first beer with her and smoked my first bowl with her. I also did my first line of coke, took my first sample of speed and had my first encounter with hashish with her. She introduced me to boys and took me to wild parties. We dabbled in the fashionable art of fad dieting, often skipping meals during the daytime only to give in to our hunger late at night. Nachos were a favorite nighttime snack for us.

At the barn, where my mom and dad assumed we under the supervision of our riding instructor – who occasionally partied with us – Amber and I would ride our horses throughout the day and hang out with the ranch hands and drink or smoke at night. My parents incorrectly assumed that my instructor, whose husband was dealing drugs and was often away, would keep us out of trouble when she let us spend the night in her trailer. She let us stay whenever we wanted to, whether she was there or not. Occasionally, her sister Kathy, who was in college, would visit and stay in the trailer with us. Kathy was beautiful, thin with blond hair and a great smile. She was also bulimic and encouraged Amber and me to try throwing up after eating. I never dreamed I would force myself to throw up, even if it meant having a thinner body. I tried it once and determined there was no way I could ever do it again. Sticking my finger down my throat burned and puking was repulsive to me. Despite the fact that I was staying up late and living the life of a college student at age 12, I was still managing to get good grades at school. Eventually, though, the combination of drugs and naïveté led me down the wrong road and into trouble.

* * *

Chapter 4 – Saying No

"I became a feminist as an alternative to becoming a masochist." – Sally Kempton

Technically, I lost my virginity with a scalpel under general anesthesia on a gurney when I was 19 in a procedure called a hymenectomy. While I didn't have a complete imperforate hymen, my opening was far too small. However, that's not to say that I was sexually inactive until that point. On the contrary, by the time I was 13, I was over the whole sexual exploration mania that most boys and girls in their teens experience. Sadly, I had grown sick of the sexual scene earlier than most, because my sexual experiences were anything but pleasant. Aside from a few tingly kisses on dares, all my sexual activity felt forced and uncomfortable. In two specific cases, they were, in fact, forced.

Most girls imagine their first time with a boy as something magical and sweet. Their dream is of two people sharing a moment, connecting on a new level and expressing a deep and profound love for one another. Unfortunately, this is hardly the typical scenario. The Centers for Disease Control and Prevention has documented that approximately 30 percent of 17-year-old girls whose first sexual intercourse was forced did not report it as such.

At first, I thought it was great to be running with the popular crowd in junior high. I had new friends who accepted and liked me based on our mutual use of recreational drugs. My newfound friends and I also thought it was terribly cool to drink, even though most of us were underage. Wherever there was a big party or gathering that involved kegs, pot or pills, we were bound to be found. At the barn where my new best friend Amber and I rode, we were able to get our hands on all kinds of mood-altering substances from the people around us. Our riding instructor smoked weed with us, the workers offered us alcohol, and what we couldn't find there, we brought with us from other sources. It was easy to find someone selling something in my hometown of Boulder. During one of our typical weekend evenings after a day of riding and cleaning out stalls, Amber and I found ourselves ingesting speed and drinking beer with the much older and very-good-looking men who were employed as ranch hands. Devin, the blacksmith, was, in my eyes, the most impressive of the bunch. Not only was he good-looking, he was also fit and fun, and just happened to be flirting with me! It didn't really strike me as odd that this guy was 26 while I was a mere 13. All I cared about was that someone as handsome as him was paying attention to me. It also didn't seem out of the ordinary when he led me away from the group and kissed me out in the fields.

When he asked if I wanted to have sex, I didn't say a word. To be honest, I wasn't sure. I was 13 and very curious, but not at all sure if I was ready. He then asked if I would rather have oral sex instead. I didn't know what that meant. He took my inability to speak at the moment as an unspoken agreement to venture forward rather than recognize it as simple confusion on my part over what his question really meant. I wasn't afraid of him or anything; he wasn't the type to hurt anyone. I was just naïve and didn't know what to say.

The situation only started to worry me when we

were naked on the waterbed inside my instructor's trailer, and, instead of feeling the pleasure of intercourse that I had somewhat anticipated or at least hoped for, I was feeling tremendous pain. After enduring the pain of him repeatedly trying to penetrate, I started to resist. It seemed obvious to me that something was wrong. I was no expert, but this couldn't be what all the hype around sex was about, and if it was, I wanted no part of it. He seemed unresponsive to my voiceless pleas to stop. Pulling away was not working, so I finally activated my vocal cords. I said "stop." He didn't. Maybe he thought I was acting a part. I said it several times more, and tried several variations on the word in case one of those might be the secret that would work. However "don't," "wait," "please stop," and even cries of pain all failed to have an effect. Finally, I became altogether rational about the situation and decided I must appeal to his intellectual side in order to make him stop, so as calmly as I could, I said, "You know this is rape, don't you?" Finally, that got him to stop. Without a word, he got up, got dressed and left. Oddly, I was overcome with a horrible sense of guilt. I felt rejected and depressed. I don't think he was intentionally trying to rape me or hurt me; it was just a very unfortunate and confusing situation. Of course now I realize how very wrong it was for a 26-year-old to be making sexual advances toward girl so young, but at the time, I experienced only overwhelming guilt.

I carried this growing guilt around with me for

several days. I was completely embarrassed about what had happened and didn't know how to handle the current state of affairs. I remember distinctly that I only ate two carrots the day after it happened. I felt fat and disgusted with myself, so the hunger pangs eased the bad feelings to some extent. Like some enlightenment seeker's strange form of self-flagellation, I tried to focus on resisting any temptation to eat. Of course, this didn't last long, and I was back to eating fairly normally in a day or two, but I was still depressed as the scenario replayed itself over and over in my head.

Devin and I continued to see each other from time to time out at the barn. I couldn't believe that I was still attracted to a guy that I felt had taken advantage of me, but I was. We avoided each other like the opposite poles of a magnet, yet both of us clearly acknowledged, awkwardly and without words, what had happened. We never talked about the incident. In fact, we rarely talked at all, but I could feel a bond between us. This strange connection was probably the result of unresolved guilt on his part as well as mine, but it managed to make me feel even more miserable over what had happened and especially about my part in it. I often mistakenly took responsibility for things beyond my control, but I honestly felt that I was at fault in this situation.

I wish I could say that this experience led me to change my ways, clean up my act, quit doing drugs or at least say no. It seemed like all the positive influence that riding had given me was shot down in a moment by my own poor judgment and inability to say no with conviction. I was left feeling even more unsure of myself than before I started riding. Unfortunately, my self-confidence would take one more blow, a blow that would have such an impact on me that it would eventually completely change who I was.

* * *

Chapter 5 -A New Me

"Feminism is the radical notion that women are people." – Cheris Kramarae and Paula Treichler

Cynthia Pfeffer, M.D. of Columbia University stated in 2004 that four to eight percent of adolescents suffer from some form of major depression. That percentage increases to 20 by the time a child reaches the age of 18. Often, teens are tempted to self-medicate, and I was no exception. Following the date rape, my drug use hardly waned; if anything, it increased. I was slowly becoming numb to the world. My developing "I don't care" attitude reached all areas of my life, except school. No matter how much I was self-destructing in the world outside school, I always managed to finish my homework and complete exams with flying colors. I was determined to prove to my dad that I was not, as he so harshly put it, retarded. A's and B's filled my report card, yet he still called me stupid. There was no winning with him. As a result, our relationship became more strained than it had already been, and I began to feel true hatred for him. Some therapists and doctors have suggested that being raped caused me to transfer my anger at the perpetrator to men in general. To me, it just unleashed the hatred I had bottled up for so many years onto a man who had continually let me down and criticized me and those around me. In reality, it was a little of both. There was also this idea that my father hadn't protected me from the world, though I never felt he was to blame in this particular case. Whatever my thoughts at the time, my anger toward him was obvious.

A few months after school let out, Amber and I discovered that the band the Rolling Stones was going to be playing in Boulder. Even though I had just finished 8th grade, I was allowed to go to the big concert without a chaperone. Amber and I decided to camp out to get tickets. It was midnight when we left my house to walk the few miles to the ticket office. We had told my parents we would leave early in the morning but sneaked out without anyone knowing. I remember being a little on edge because the two of us were on our favorite drug of choice, speed, and we had just seen the movie *An American Werewolf in*

London.

When we arrived at the ticket office, there were already quite a few people in line. Several of Amber's high-school friends approached us and offered us some unknown type alcohol in a brown paper bag. Before I knew it, I was separated from the herd and alone with some random guy. For some reason, virtually everything about that night is still very clear in my mind today, yet I can't remember at all what this guy looked like. I think he had dark hair. I wasn't paying attention to a word he was saying, because I was busy trying to figure out where Amber had gone. I kept looking around, but just could not see her. The guy asked if I wanted to go for a ride in his new car. "I have to find my friend," I blurted, and took off.

After much searching, I finally found Amber and told her about this guy. She told me I should go, that the guy probably liked me. She was clearly busy chatting it up with not one but two guys. Torn between my own needs and trying to please others, my choice ended up being a dangerous one. Reluctantly, I sought out the guy and said, "Ok, I'll go for a ride." I regret not following my instinct and staying put, but there was a part of me that was still desperately trying to fit in and not upset anyone.

I had a bad feeling in my stomach the entire time that he took my hand and walked me to his car. My sixth sense picked up on something ominous in the air that night. He opened the door for me, and I got in. He drove toward the mountains and made small talk as I grew increasingly more worried. I kept thinking what an idiot I was. This was so unsafe and I knew it. As he talked, I examined the car door, trying to figure out how to escape should the need arise. When he finally parked the car in an isolated parking lot near the base of the Foothills, I considered running. I imagined opening the door and just running away, but there was a side of me that was afraid. Where would I go? I'd be alone, far from my friend and far from home. What would this guy do? Would he come after me? Would he just leave me up there alone?

He asked me if I had ever given anyone a blowjob. I said no. He asked if I knew how to give one. Again, I said no. Without another word, he unzipped his pants, grabbed the back of my neck and instructed me on the proper blowjob technique. I was disgusted when he came in my mouth, but relieved as he leaned over, opened the door and allowed me to spit.

The door! Oh God, the door. I had forgotten about my escape plan. The fresh air felt good on my face. I spit the gum I was chewing out too, and thought how gross it was that I hadn't spit it out before. Had I known what he'd had in store, I might have thought ahead. I assumed the worst part was over, so I leaned back and allowed him to close the door. We drove back to the ticket office in silence, and regrouped with the others in line. I was shocked at what had just happened. When I pulled Amber aside and told her about what had occurred, her response saddened me.

"Oh, gross," was all she said. No words of comfort or concern.

The numbness in me grew. How had I let this happen?

I tossed the incident over and over in my mind until I was sick of it. The drugs and alcohol were wearing off and I was becoming more aware of myself. Amber and I bought our tickets and parted ways. As I was walking to the bus stop for a ride home, I felt a surge of energy and hope. Then, in an instant, I decided to change. My life was going to be different. I was going to take control. I put forth an intention out into the universe that was so loud and clear, so heartfelt and determined that it couldn't be denied. I was going on a diet!

* * *

Chapter 6 – Tricks of the Trade

"Nothing would be more tiresome than eating and drinking if God had not made them a pleasure as well as a necessity." – Voltaire

Almost everyone has little food quirks that make eating more enjoyable. My friend used to eat the chocolate off her Butterfinger candy bar first instead of biting directly into it, savoring the peanut-butter-flavored inside like some edible treasure she had just unburied. Another friend of mine uses this chocolate removal process on ice cream bars. It has become a tradition to either open up an Oreo cookie and lick away, or use the teeth to scrape out, the creamy filling, or dunk the cookie in milk. These little habits we form are all quite normal and do make eating a fun experience. An anorexic, on the other hand, takes this food-play to an abnormal extreme, and any ritual around food moves away from fun or playful into unpleasant territory. These kinds of obsessive actions have a different flavor than the enjoyment of, say, stacking several Pringles potato chips together before chomping down. For example, one of my friends who suffered from anorexia cut up a turkey sandwich into small cubes. Over the course of three days, she'd slowly consume nothing but these tiny cubes, one at a sitting. One girl I knew ate chewable vitamins for dessert. The most extreme game I encountered didn't actually involve food but rather extreme deprivation. A friend of mine, whom I met in the hospital, grew increasingly afraid to swallow her own saliva. She refused any solid food and all liquids, and spit into a cup that she carried around with her. It did not take long for her to be rushed to the medical unit when she passed out from dehydration.

The term anorexia was essentially unheard of among my friends when I was 13. However, anorexia was documented and described as far back as the

1700s, and there is evidence suggesting that anorexia may have existed far earlier than this. Many famous women, including the long-suffering English writer Virginia Woolf, may have been anorexic, but didn't openly admit their secret battles with food. Unfortunately, anorexia today seems to be not only more visible in the general public, but virtually celebrated in the world of models and celebrities. The pithy homily "you can never be too rich or too thin" ignores that fact that many people can, in fact, be too thin, with lethal consequences for some of them.

My initial decision to go on a diet was part of an entire transformation into a new being. Although it was no religious revelation, it had similar characteristics in that I wanted to be pure. I was on a mission to purge myself of the guilt of merely existing, a burden I experienced on a daily basis. As part of this process, I gave up drugs, drinking and smoking, partaking in any of these vices only extremely rarely as opposed to every weekend.

At first, during the summer before 9th grade, I decided to just improve my eating habits a little bit. I became a salad-bar hound, and tuna fish was a new diet staple. I wanted to be more normal, noting that there were plenty of people in the world who ate three meals a day who were skinny, so it made sense that I could do the same. For me, three meals a day meant absolutely no snacks, no matter how hungry I was. I soon found that I liked the challenge of being hungry, so over the next few weeks, I gave myself harder and harder challenges around food deprivation and quickly tossed out any traditional dieting regimes. Eventually, I settled into a month-long diet of peanut butter, bagels and milk. Twice a day, I would split open a large bagel, toast the two halves, scoop a few heaping tablespoons of peanut butter topped with large mounds of my mom's homemade strawberry jam onto each, and sit down to eat with a large glass of milk. After a month of this, I was visibly thinner, and hungry for bigger challenges. One day I ate a very large bowl of popcorn very, very slowly. This and a glass of orange juice were all I consumed for the day. Another day I sucked on a small bag of frozen grapes for breakfast and ate a small dinner and an ice cream cone for dessert.

It became overly obvious that this dieting was more about control than looking good or feeling healthy when my mom, frantic at the sight of her little girl wasting away, forced me to sit and eat a soft boiled egg. She screamed at me to eat the goddamned egg until I was sobbing at the table. She wouldn't allow me to leave until I had finished the egg, so I choked it down and promptly threw up in the bathroom. She may have won the battle, but I was determined to win the war, no matter what the sacrifice. Because my mom knew I had puked up the egg, she didn't fight me on eating again. She knew I was sick, but she wasn't able to act in a way that would curtail my self-destructive behavior. I suppose she felt it better that I keep the little bit I did eat down than risk me throwing up everything she forced me to eat. I did eat ice cream regularly, so she filled the freezer for me in an attempt to keep me alive. Because I was becoming so thin, foods that were once off-limits became acceptable for me. This was my ice cream, and all hell would break loose if anyone else ate it.

In addition to my over-the-top dieting, I designed my own little exercise program. Several times a week I would half-walk and half-jog a 1.5-mile hilly loop that started and ended at my house. I also rode my bike to the park with a book in my backpack to read, so I could keep my mind occupied and off the hunger pangs until my next small meal. Often I would read for what seemed like an eternity only to look at my watch and find that only a few short minutes had passed. For a while, I continued horseback riding, but used it as a new form of calorie burning. I no longer had the desire to show or improve as a rider. Often I tried to increase the times I could ride around the arena without stirrups at a posting trot, just to burn ever more calories. After one last horse show that summer, my sister and I found ourselves with less and less time to ride. Both of us were too busy with other activities and preparing for school, so shortly after we started classes, we made the painful decision to sell Michelob. Both of us quit riding all together once our formerly treasured horse was gone. Much later, after my sister moved away, got married and had children, she took it up again. It's one sport that I still miss. I rode briefly again many years later when I was about 35 years old, attempting to learn dressage like my sister, but I wasn't able to keep up the lessons with my schedule. Being able to ride a stubborn but cute little Fjord Pony after years of being away from this activity brought me great joy. I was sad when I had to face the fact that riding no longer fit into my lifestyle.

I entered ninth grade a full 30 pounds lighter than when I'd left school the previous spring. Some of the other students thought I was a new student at first, because they didn't recognize my new, extremely thin body. I had gone back to a very strict routine of three meals a day and dessert after dinner with no snacks in between in an attempt to be more normal, at least in outward behavior. My new game was to see how small I could make my meals. At 95 lbs, my weight was still dropping as I left a longer and longer trail of sandwich pieces for the birds that I hoped my friends wouldn't notice as we walked back to school from the deli at lunchtime. I tried to hide the fact that I was so thin and had these weird eating habits, but at 95 lbs on a 5'3" frame didn't look healthy. People began to talk.

In a sense, I was a new person. The year before, I had qualified for the varsity basketball team. I was a fierce guard with a strong talent for interceptions and stealing the ball. I was also accepted into Madrigals, a small, unaccompanied singing group. However, the next year, my senior year in junior high, I was frail and weak. In my first basketball game, my teammate nearly knocked me over with a hard pass. The ball felt overly heavy in my arms. I spent most of the season on the bench. In Madrigals, I was timid and my voice not nearly as powerful as the year before. Oddly, even though I felt weaker in these events, I felt more confident overall.

I was convinced I looked good, despite the horror of knowing that my hair was thinning at an alarming rate and I could see my ribs. On some level, I knew I was thin, but I couldn't see exactly how thin. I assumed I looked fairly normal. Just before I hit 90 pounds, my schoolmate Danielle invited me to go running with her on our lunch break. She was a cross-country skier training for the upcoming ski season. I immediately jumped at the thought of a great new way to burn more calories. I had run track the year before but was slow and only managed a painfully executed 8-minute mile. Danielle and I met every day and ran two miles. I wore basketball shoes and baggy sweat pants. Even when the weather was terrible – rainy, or cold and snowing – the two of us would find ourselves enduring the elements, proud of what dedicated athletes we were. With not getting the proper nutrition and my low body fat, I was cold all the time and on days we took on the snow, I often couldn't work my frozen hands after the run. Several times I had to get help from one of the other girls in the locker room undressing and dressing, so that I could get to my next class in time.

Ultimately and without knowing it, Danielle may have offered me a new direction in life, because instead of a goal of how many more pounds I could lose, my new goal became how fast I could run. No one could know at the time what that would unleash, both good and bad.

Danielle reminded me that food was fuel. We indulged ourselves in ice cream every night, convincing ourselves that we deserved it after all the hard training we had done. When we went to the movies, we would sneak in an entire pint of Ben and Jerry's to eat during the previews. I still had all the compulsive eating habits of a nutty anorexic, like absolutely no snacks and limiting my intake, but I managed to gain a few pounds and settled at around 95-98 pounds for the remainder of the year. I weighed myself at least once a day to make sure that my weight never got over the 100-pound mark. There were episodes during the most agonizing periods of my illness where I would compulsively weigh myself multiple times a day. The most important thing that happened at the time I was in junior high, though, was finding a new sport.

* * *

Chapter 7 -Running on Empty

"Tough times don't last but tough people do." – A.C. Green

I struggled with anorexia for over 20 years. Throughout this long battle I had periods of relative health and periods of severe illness, but what is most surprising is that for approximately eight of those years, I was one of the top runners in the nation, setting records and winning races around the country. Though I survived, my story isn't pretty, and I suffered long-term consequences from starving myself while training intensely.

Training without proper nutrition can lead to many complications, yet it's common for athletes to restrict their nutritional intake in order to achieve a lighter weight. According to world-renowned running coach Bobby McGee: "From a plain exercise physiological point of view, the lighter the runner, the higher their VO2 Max. This is their ability (measured in milliliters) to utilize oxygen per kilogram of body weight. This is a key performance factor in endurance events. The lighter the athlete, therefore, the better they perform – hence the warped 'reward' that these athletes receive for losing so much weight. Of course this period of heightened performance is finite as the effects of the illness start to shut down the system with its all too often inevitable outcome – terrible, terrible illness, anguish and even death."

In addition, he states, "Athletes I have worked with over the last 25 years have displayed a myriad of conditions: ketosis, where the athlete begins to metabolize their own tissue (protein) for energy; dysmenorrheal, where the regular menstrual cycle becomes erratic, possibly due to too little body fat (I see the cut off at around 13%); amenorrhea, where bleeding ceases all together, which leads to losses in bone density, stress fractures, and eventual osteoporosis. There is obviously a great deal of mental and emotional stress in both the short term and the long term. The possible replacement of the eating disorder with an exercise addiction can also alter the nature of the situation psychologically."

Bobby is clear that the long-term effects can be persistent and extremely detrimental. He further states, "The ability that the athlete displayed as a result of an increased VO2 Max due to weight loss in the early stages is rarely regained fully. The focus becomes the disease and the running a fantasy that harks back to a time when the condition was insufficiently advanced to warn those able to help." According to Bobby, it is also evident that women can suffer erratic menstrual cycles and ill health long after normal eating habits have been restored. The "female triad," the condition to which Bobby alludes, is a term coined by The American College of Sports Medicine that comprises three conditions: disordered eating, amenorrhea, and the loss of bone density, or osteoporosis, with the first two derangements leading to the third. The body is resilient, but not immune to self-abuse, especially the longer the abuse continues. If an athlete continually trains or overtrains on too little nutrition, it's possible she may never return to normal health.

At the time I was running well, I felt indestructible.

The thought of a compromised body or ill heath later in life never crossed my mind. As with any addict, even if I had some concept of what life might be like, I was too caught up in my compulsive behavior to truly grasp the possible outcome. Like a rebel teen who knows that smoking can cause lung cancer but does it anyway, I was too dedicated to my addiction to change my path. There were people who tried to warn me that I was heading down a dangerous road, but I refused to listen. The addiction was feeding something lacking in me. My running success gave me the attention I didn't get growing up, and the compulsions distracted me from my past. Though I did suffer several minor injuries early in my career, such as a pulled Achilles tendon and several sprained ankles, I didn't consider the long-term consequences of what starvation can do to the body. My sole purpose in life was to run and feed my addiction of eating a certain way while exercising intensely. Despite knowing some basic physiology of the human body, it seemed impossible that I could actually die from not eating enough. In the end, I came close to dying, but I was fortunate enough to survive. Whether it was my will to live that eventually made an appearance or something out of my hands that caused me to last, I consider myself lucky in terms of remaining on the planet.

In March 2006, Alex DeVinny, the 2003 Wisconsin state champion in the 3200-meter run, died from cardiac arrest related to anorexia. She was 5 feet 8 inches tall and weighed around 70 pounds at the time of her death. In a September 14, 2004 *New York Times* article, "When Being Varsity-Fit Masks an Eating Disorder," author Paul Scott addresses the tough position a coach can be put in when it comes to girls and running. He states, "Looking back, her coach, Dan Jarrett, questions himself. 'I did not understand how someone with anorexia would be capable of making decisions that weren't in their best interest,' he said. 'I totally failed to grasp what it meant.' He is so troubled by her death that he has since quit coaching girls."

Former Fairview High School cross country and track coach Joanne Ernst knows first-hand how difficult recognizing and treating eating disorders in runners can be. In an interview, she expressed her concerns as a coach. "It's difficult to know how to intervene," Joanne admits. "There is new science today that helps confront the issue, but the information is still changing." Often, eating disorders such as bulimia can go undetected by a coach. In Joanne's case, she was lucky to have relatively few runners who suffered from an eating disorder in her years of coaching at the high-school level. When Joanne did encounter one athlete who was visibly too thin, she had a talk with the girl's mother and suggested that the girl not join the team until she was at a more reasonable weight.

In general, to help runners avoid injuries and other running-related issues, Joanne had a just a few simple rules that she had learned from her own experience as a professional athlete. Number one: Comments about weight were to be avoided. Good nutrition was emphasized, but there was no exact diet given or ideal weight mentioned. And number two: The running program was not based on high mileage. Instead, it was more about quality training, covering the basics of good training and nothing more. With the help of several assistant coaches, Joanne ran a very successful running program for eight years.

The job of a coach is not an easy one. A good coach relies on open, honest communication with his athletes. If the information given is skewed, coaches are not able to make sound decisions regarding the appropriate kind of training for their athletes. For an athlete with an eating disorder, it's common to bend the truth. Lies about how much training is taking place are the most common breach of trust in the coach-athlete relationship. Food intake and actual weight can be an issue as well. Scott also addresses this issue in his article: "Even the best-trained psychologist can have a difficult time filtering through the deceptive acts and statements that can accompany an eating disorder. And yet coaches have long been encouraged to identify a syndrome of under-eating, known as the female athlete triad, to help athletes avoid osteoporosis, stress fractures and – in rare cases like Ms. DeVinny's – even death." Unfortunately, most coaches are neither equipped to deal with identifying the specific symptoms that lead to the female triad, nor trained to detect the deceitful acts in which anorexics engage. By the time I entered high school, I had already been anorexic for over a year, so I was very good at deception. Most people had no idea what kind of struggles with food I had. They assumed I was thin because I ran, not because I was afraid to eat. Running was something I did so that I didn't feel so guilty about eating. In the end, I allowed myself the reward of eating because I ran; even though I understood intellectually that the body needs caloric intake even at rest, I couldn't embrace it on an emotional level.

* * *

Chapter 8 –The Running Years

"To give anything less than the best is to

sacrifice the gift." -Steve Prefontaine

Janis Joplin once said the only time she ever felt beautiful was when she was on stage singing. Often, one can find beauty by living in the moment. In doing this, we are offered a way to forget ourselves. We can feel weightless and have no thoughts of the future or past, experiencing the world at large and connecting to the universe. When we move past our calling into compulsion, though, the beauty is lost.

I placed fourth in the women's division in my first road race, a two-miler, one mile uphill and the other down. I was 14 years old at the time. Just a few months before the race, I had started running with Danielle. By the time spring rolled around, I was eager to run track. Danielle and I quickly proved to be the top athletes on the team and even led track practices every now and then. Despite my terrible hunger and occasional weakness from not eating enough, we made running fun. We often led the team through drills, stopping to do a few crazy somersaults on the grass as the rest of the team stood nearby and wondered whether or not they should follow suit.

Danielle was a muscular 800-meter runner with great strength, and I was a lanky long-distance runner. The two of us trained in the hills, running on dirt trails and venturing out into the wilderness. We had several basic two- or three-mile loops that we ran and occasionally ran as far as five miles. I would eventually settle on the longest race available in junior high school, the mile. In a short time, I had developed a passion for running that was unstoppable. My inability to hold back almost cost me a friendship, when I agreed to run a race with a friend and couldn't resist the urge to charge ahead and leave her behind. Fortunately the girl understood that my love of racing was too strong to be harnessed. Like a racehorse, I couldn't wait to get into the middle of the competition, and when I tried my first mile run in practice, I busted out a six-minute-flat performance completely alone. The coach was impressed. At the end of the year, Danielle won the 800 and I set a new district record in the mile by running just under six minutes. Later that spring, I ran a 10-kilometer road race on a challenging course in around 40 minutes. All of a sudden I was known as "the runner," and high-school coaches were swarming around me.

During the summer after graduating from junior high school, I received letters from the two main high schools in Boulder: Fairview High and Boulder High. Both coaches wanted me to run for their cross-country team. I was flattered and couldn't wait to join a team and have a new coach. I opted for Fairview mostly because all of my siblings had gone there, and a few people I knew around the neighborhood had also attended. Danielle was accepted to a private high school in the mountains, so we agreed to keep in touch by writing letters and visiting on holidays. I was sad to see her leave, but at the same time I was looking forward to a new school and the chance to compete on a well-known high-school running team.

Without my knowledge, my parents had gone to talk to the coach at Fairview out of concern that I was too thin and training too much. He assured them that his training methods were reasonable and safe. He let them know he would watch out for me. At the time, I was running about 20 to 30 miles a week. Eventually I would develop full-blown anorexia athletica in which running, a preoccupation with food and diet, and compulsive rituals would rule my world. Anorexia athletica in distance runners sometimes goes undetected, because it's common to see very thin people in the sport. In general, those who suffer from anorexia athletica often no longer enjoy their exercise, and feel obligated to perform. Before I reached this desperate state, though, I loved my sport.

During my first season of cross-country it immediately became apparent that I was the fastest girl on the team. I respected my teammates, idolized my new coach and wanted nothing more than to please everyone by running well. Being a people-pleaser is not uncommon for anorexics. I knew my coach was experienced and had coached other successful runners. He found that my strength was long distance. He bumped my mileage up to 40 to 50 miles per week. I often trained with the boys' team and quickly became a running sensation. As a newcomer, I was undefeated in races. I even made waves in co-ed races. My greatest joy was competing against boys and showing them who was boss. One of my favorite events was a small meet in which teams had to choose three runners, including at least one girl. Our team did a first-through-third-place sweep, with me placing third overall. In general, I was modest and shy and very afraid of failure, but once I got on the track or cross-country course, I was free and at one with my body. However, just as I was discovering this wild new power in me and embracing my rebellious side with a "fuck you" attitude, I was slowly becoming more compulsive about both my training and my eating.

Once I started winning races, the newspapers were all over my story. Unfortunately, it meant that some of my private life spilled into public view. Without realizing that an "off the record" comment meant that it could still end up in print, I was a little too forthcoming with information. The day after my interview for the local paper, I saw in bold headlines that anorexia had led me to running. My secret was out, but I was doing my best to keep the fact that I was struggling under wraps. I had a military-style routine that was strict and disciplined. I woke up at 5 a.m. every day for a small breakfast and calisthenics. I had a small sore on my back from doing sit-ups on the carpet – I didn't have enough meat on my bones to protect my lower back. After exercising, I rode my bike to school carrying only a skimpy sandwich for lunch, had track practice after school, then rode my bike home for an early dinner that was the same every single day: a small portion of chicken, vegetables with low-fat dressing, and two cookies with an enormous amount of ice cream (I'm afraid to think how thin I would have been had it not been for the large quantity of ice cream I consumed). Any straying from my routine caused me great upset and sometimes resulted in tantrums. These included excessive frowning, stomping around the house and occasionally yelling. Again my parents approached my coach and begged him to intervene. He looked them square in the eye and said, "Well, she must be doing something right, because she's winning races." At first, my parents, who had my best interests in mind, thought my coach could be their ally and might talk some sense into me. At this point, however, they knew they had lost any chance of reaching or rescuing me.

The more my parents suggested healthy eating and moderation in training, the greater the conflict between us became. I looked up to my coach and began to distrust everything my parents said. My destiny was running, and I wasn't going to tolerate anything that threatened to get in the way of that future. Strangely enough, it was only when I became a good runner that I got some respect from my father for what I felt was the first time ever. He seemed proud, yet my anger at him only increased. I became a bit of a prima donna. I was demanding and grumpy before races and wasn't afraid to take out my stress on my dad by glaring at him or simply being rude. To everyone else, I was sweet and kind. Nobody knew how deep my anger ran.

By the end of my very first cross-country season, as a sophomore, I was feeling the pressure. On the day of the state meet, I was bleeding from the rectum from eight small ulcers that were forming and would go undetected until I was in my twenties. I would develop severe bleeding hemorrhoids later in life due to so much straining, not only in an attempt to clear my colon before a run, but due to incorrect breathing and extreme physical effort in general. I tearfully stood on the starting line, pale and 98 pounds. After a slow start, I found my stride, but it was too late and I ended up fifth. Although I vowed to do better the following spring, track season was a repeat of cross-country. After an undefeated regular season, I lost the state meet by placing second in the 3200 meters, just behind a girl who outkicked me in the last 100 meters. It seemed unfair that she sat on my tail the entire way, only to sprint past me at the very end. I wasn't used to tactical racing. I broke down and cried on the infield. I didn't care that the cameras were on me; it felt as if my life were over. No amount of consoling could ease my disappointment.

A few days later, I had an epiphany and decided I would never let such a thing happen again. I needed to train harder and become the best; that was all there was to it. Once again I vowed to become more dedicated. I wouldn't get caught up in someone else's race and was driven to run the way I wanted.

Already I had become somewhat antisocial, not eating at food-related events, avoiding going out with others and training mostly alone. My increased determination to succeed in running caused me to become isolated from the team, and saw me training more on my own and avoiding team activities. My teammates tried in vain to include me in fun runs to the ice-cream store and other social events, but I politely refused. I didn't even go in the restaurant when the team stopped to get a bite after one cross-country race. Instead, I waited in the car while the team had fun eating and socializing inside. My mind was on races to come, and I was convinced I had to keep training harder in order to win them. Nothing was going to get in my way, certainly not an easy run to get snacks with friends when I could be doing a long, hard trail run.

The summer before my junior year brought ample opportunities to partake in road races. Before summer even arrived, my coach put me on a program to get me ready for the Bolder Boulder, held every year on Memorial Day and one of the biggest 10-kilometer road races in the country. I did mile repeats and intervals more suited for my endurance-based talent. I was much more in my element with the longer races, and popped a low 36-minute 10k at 5,300' altitude for a ninth-place overall finish in one of the largest races in the United States. I was running with the big girls now, and I was ready for it.

At age 16, I was becoming a fierce competitor on the roads, but I also had my eye on the mountains. One race in particular intrigued me – the Pikes Peak

Ascent. This August race starts at the base of a mountain with a peak that lies more than 14,000 feet above sea level and climbs 13.32 miles to the top. My coach agreed to help me train. With a huge increase in mileage and remaining dead-set on controlling my food intake, I saw my weight abruptly plummet to 92 pounds. Strangely, I felt strong and confident. My life soon revolved around the race. Severe bloody blisters on my feet and worsening fatigue every morning did nothing to deter me. My training times were remarkable and I could hardly wait to get to the starting line. I spent so much time in preparation for the race that I never once considered what would happen after the event. All I could visualize was getting to the top of that mountain as fast as possible.

With a few more road races under my belt and countless hours of training behind me, I ran the race of a lifetime, a race that was dreamlike in nature and left me in a heap at the top of the mountain. I collapsed into the arms of race officials, hyperventilating and nearly passing out as my foot crossed the line, setting a new women's record. Two hours and thirty-nine minutes after I had started, I became the youngest women's winner of the Ascent, and shortly afterward, I was placed on a stretcher and given oxygen, my legs aching and my chest burning. I was smiling, though, knowing I had reached my goal. Race officials were alarmed at my thin appearance and, perhaps with me in mind, established a still-standing rule that nobody under the age of 16 could enter the race. They were convinced that the race was too grueling. As for me, sitting on top of the mountain with my biggest victory yet, I had no idea that soon I would be heading over the edge. It wasn't my young age that was alarming; it was the illness that was slowly swallowing my life.

* * *

Chapter 9 – Women in Sports

"Because I am a woman, I must make unusual efforts to succeed. If I fail, no one will say, "She doesn't have what it takes." They will say, "Women don't have what it takes." - – Clare Boothe Luce

In 1966, Roberta Gibb became the first woman to run the Boston Marathon, but she had to do it unofficially and anonymously by hiding in the bushes before the race and jumping in among the men once the race started. A year later, the year I was born, Katherine Switzer officially ran the race under the name K. Switzer, using the initial to disguise her gender. She ran with a small group of men alongside her who had to protect her from physical attack from outraged protesters and race officials, who felt that women shouldn't be running. Oddly enough, in 1959,

Arlene Pieper became the first woman to officially finish a marathon in the United States when she crossed the finish line of the Pikes Peak Marathon, one of the most difficult marathons in the world. Her time up and down the mountain was 9:16. There was no doubt that women could go the distance. They had been doing it for years, but proving that to the rest of the world would be a problem, even eight years later, when Switzer was nearly shoved off the Boston Marathon course by a race official.

In the early eighties, when I started my running career, women's running was still a relatively new sport. The first women's Olympic marathon had yet to be run and the women's steeplechase would not even be considered as an Olympic spectator sport for another 20 years. Although running bras had been invented, they wouldn't be widely available until a few years later. In general, most women I knew wore normal everyday lace bras for training. Consumer-level heart-rate monitors were not used and running watches were very basic; there were no altimeters, GPS systems or mapping software. Running tights were new to the scene, and though running shoes were not the hard-leather contraptions my grandfather wore for running, they were far from the high-tech creations they are today.

Athletes such as the late Norwegian superstar Grete Waitz and New Zealand running legend Lorraine Moller – who would one day settle in Boulder, miles from where I make my home today –

were track and cross-country runners before they broke ground in the marathon. Eventually they would prove that women could not only run, but run well. Greta won the New York City Marathon a remarkable nine times. In addition, she set a world record four out of those nine times. She became the first woman to break the 2:30 barrier in the marathon and she rightly became a legend in her own time. Lorraine, who started running at the age of fourteen, would eventually win the Olympic Bronze medal in the marathon. In ultramarathons, women proved their true strength by running with the men, and, in some cases, beating them. Still, women were not always treated with the respect they deserved, and even in my own experiences it was not uncommon to be tripped, pushed or cut off by a male runner in a race.

When I began my running, there was no shortage of heroes for me to look up to in the sport. In the beginning I admired the famous Prefontaine and followed his motto of always giving everything possible all the time. For him it worked. For me, this meant training and racing hard, going all out from the start to the finish of a race and never settling for a slow pace in order to attempt to outkick someone. Later I learned that this was a rookie mistake often made by runners who don't have faith that they will be able to dig deep when needed. It's as if they have to prove to themselves and those around them that they are number one in every race, training session and interval. This method of training wears on both the body and the spirit. The true standouts of distance running are those who can back off at the right times and push harder when it counts.

The other idols that I had at the time in addition to Waitz included outstanding Portuguese distance runner Rosa Mota; barefoot South African sensation Zola Budd, who would become entangled in controversy in the 1984 Olympics; and the incredible track star Mary Decker (now Mary Slaney) from the United States. Lorraine, as I mentioned, is originally from New Zealand but lived and trained in Boulder during much of her career. She was not only a great athlete and an inspiration to me and many others, but a wildly powerful thinker with a heart as big as the sky. Never once did her success and fame as an Olympic athlete get in the way of her reaching out to others, myself included. She was someone who was never afraid to offer counsel, be it running-related or lifestyle-related. Over time, Lorraine went from being someone I idolized to a friend.

When I sat down to interview Lorraine for this book, I wondered what her take on eating disorders would be. I knew that she had never fallen completely into any eating disorder. While it's common for elite runners to be lean and fit, it's highly unlikely that anyone starving herself will achieve long-term success in the sport. It's not unheard of for runners to watch their weight during race season, but it's impossible to compete well on an empty gas tank. It's a fine line between being race fit and being too thin. Given the intensity of marathon running, I figured that Lorraine had at least some idea of what it was all about. In addition, her time spent as an elite athlete and later as a coach surely had allowed her to encounter others with eating issues.

I learned right away that many other great thinkers share Lorraine's beliefs concerning self-esteem. Self-regard and the ability to believe in ourselves affect all areas of our lives, even health. The more we understand ourselves, the more likely we're able to move through illness and hard times without getting stuck. For Lorraine, illness is a matter of degree. "We work through illness as a means to better understand ourselves," she says. "There is a complex set of circumstances and other factors that impact our ability to stay well." Though Lorraine admits that she may have had shades of an eating disorder at various times in her life, she never gave in fully to the illness. "It was going through these hard times that allowed me to come to terms with it and grow," she says. "I feel that the very qualities that led me to overcome these struggles are also what led me to be at the top of my sport." During her long career in running – which started at age seventeen when she fist represented New Zealand in international races and went on to include a remarkable four Olympic Marathons, the last at age 43 – she noted that other women who did succumb to anorexia may have had brief bursts of excellence in the sport, but could not sustain success for long periods.

Lorraine was relatively lucky to have been well-coached. At the time when she began running, women were not a common sight on the track, or, for that matter, in any running races. "The term anorexia was not even coined then," she says. "The Twiggy model mindset was not yet in place. As athletes, we ate well and were healthy. There were natural fluctuations in my weight due to differences in my training, but it never became a pressing or pathological concern." Most female athletes, especially those who began competing after 1980, were not so lucky.

There's no doubt that these pioneering women athletes had a hard road. They had to overcome stereotypes and verbal abuse, and on most of them there was also the added pressure to be thin. I was anorexic even before I started running. As a result, I experienced both internal and external pressure to remain thin. Before that time, I was fat, or at least I thought I was. My entire childhood was filled with others making fun of my weight and criticizing me to no end.

People often ask me how it all started. As I see it, there was no one thing that triggered the illness; rather it was an accumulation of events that must have started from the time I was born. In reality, my illness was a coping mechanism, a way to survive. It was a way to push the pain of everyday living away. There may have been a final straw that broke the camel's back and led to the onset of my illness, but the tendency toward an eating disorder was set in motion much earlier.

* * *

Chapter 10 – On M&M's

"Worries go down better with soup." –
Jewish proverb

I was almost never sick when I was in grade
school. My mom tried everything to get me to catch
the chickenpox when a mini-epidemic was going
around our neighborhood, but no matter how many
pox-stricken children I played with, my immune
system just wouldn't allow me to join their ranks.

Years later, after anorexia had completely
compromised my body's ability to fight any illness, I
would long for those days of health. Back then,
though, I felt like I was missing out on something – the
pampering from parents that comes with being sick.
The extra attention my sister seemed to get as a child I
thought was because she was thin and pretty. I didn't
know at the time that it was really because she was so
sickly.

Although my super-powered immune system
fought off most childhood illnesses, I was unfortunately
slightly accident-prone. When I was 10, I was so used

to getting stitches that I didn't even flinch when the doctor had to repair my bloody hand after a vicious dog bite. He told my parents how brave I had been. I was only trying to prove to the world that I wasn't a baby, so I refused to cry when the doctor crammed a large amount of gauze into one of the open wounds to drain it, a procedure he later confessed had made grown men shed a few tears. By the time I was 12, nearly every body part had been stitched, bruised, broken or otherwise hurt. Some say that children who constantly have accidents are subconsciously seeking attention. I don't know that I was aware of trying to get attention at age two when my dad was drunk and supposed to be watching me. I fell, hitting my chin on a glass table, but I suppose the two stitches in my tiny chin did cause a small fuss around me. It's true that later injuries did produce several gifts, and heartfelt hugs and kisses that were normally kept at a minimum in my family, but eventually all the accidents led to people around me thinking I was faking or being a baby.

My sister, unlike me, rarely got hurt. She was, on the other hand, sick all the time. She nearly died of a kidney infection when she was four and a half. Because my sister's illness was so severe, much of my parent's attention was focused on her, while I was left to play by myself. I must have had some sense of not wanting to be a pest, because my mom declares that I was a well-behaved child who rarely cried. I was jealous of all the attention my sister got and envied all the extra goodies she seemed to accumulate from others as a result of her frail, thin appearance. Periodically, because my constitution was so damn strong, I would fake being sick so that I could stay home from school. On these occasions I would curl up in the big comfy chair we had in the kitchen and watch TV while munching on M&M's I had stolen from the top cupboard. These were the times during which I felt safe. I had sweet chocolate melting in my mouth (and under the seat cushion where the M&M's were hidden) to soothe my loneliness. Also, I was home, away from the insults of other kids. I knew the next day I would have to face it all again, but for brief moments at a time, I felt comforted and protected from the outside world. I was forever craving the nurturing and attention I lacked as a child.

At the time, I had no idea that I was seeking love through M&M's. I felt deprived; felt that I was being denied what I considered my sister's privilege. The M&M's were, in fact, meant for my sister. My parents were trying desperately to put some weight on her tiny body, while at the same time trying to keep more of it from forming on mine. Of course, early in my anorexic years, the tables would turn, and the ice cream in the freezer would be dubbed mine. Everyone knew that ice cream was one of the few things I would eat, so it was essential to have some on hand at all times. When I was little, though, at least when it came to eating, I wasn't to be trusted with my own decisions. I would eat too much or the wrong things if someone wasn't watching closely. So I felt obligated to sneak and hoard candy any time I could get my hands on it.

Geneen Roth has written several books about eating disorders. In *When Food is Love*, she tells the story of a young overweight girl whose mother was trying to prevent her from gaining more weight. Geneen suggested that the mother provide the girl with an unlimited supply of the girl's favorite food, which happened to be M&M's. At first, the girl, who carried these M&M's around in a pillowcase everywhere she went like some security blanket, gained more weight. But eventually she realized the M&M's were symbolic of her mother's love and trust. Once she realized that her mother would not try to control her food intake anymore, she no longer felt the need to carry the M&M's around. She had found solace in the fact that her mother had shown her unconditional love. Her mother had given her the M&M's despite the fact that she initially gained weight, and had reassured her that she could have M&M's whenever she wanted. The sweet treats would not be taken away from her, nor would her mother's love. I don't mean to imply that a *Lord of the Flies* scenario is optimal for raising children and that they should have free rein; I think it's more a matter of providing a child with the right balance of guidance and freedom. As a parent, I'm sure it's a difficult task to reassure a child that she will be loved no matter what. It must also be difficult to have faith that your child can learn to make the right decisions for herself.

I assume that reading the signs given by one's own body is innate. It appears to be, because babies cry when they are hungry or wet or have some other unmet basic need. However, once a child experiences emotions or conflict, these messages can easily become confused.

Anorexics are often stereotyped as high-achieving, overly sensitive and intelligent individuals. This may be true in many cases, but at our worst we become manipulative, controlling and deceitful. We don't do this on purpose. It's more a matter of survival or an attempt to keep our strange mythical world intact at all costs. An anorexic may be alternately shunned and idolized as some kind of godlike creature who is able to deny herself the most basic of needs: food. Somewhere along the way, though, it becomes obvious that we lose the ability to trust our own hunger, our own bodies and our own needs. The longer this denial continues, the more out of touch we become with both our bodies and all aspects of reality. When my illness was ruling my life, I never actually had any sense of my bodily needs. I had no idea what it felt like to be hungry or full. I knew empty, but I didn't realize at the time that empty was very different from hungry. As a young child, I had been using food emotionally to help ease the bad feelings of loneliness and sadness. While food temporarily made me feel better, it had no lasting effect and ultimately made the situation worse by adding pounds to my already chubby body. Later, I found a new way to distract myself from the bad feelings, a way that nearly killed me.

* * *

Chapter 11 – The Making of an Anorexic

"The young always have the same problem – how to rebel and conform at the same time. They have now solved this by defying their parents and copying one another." – Quentin Crisp

Because I felt out of place as a child and assumed that nobody liked me or wanted to be around me because I was fat, I became a bit of a loner. In my eyes, people didn't ever like me, they just tolerated me.

While I was fortunate to have a mother who was always there for me, I ended up relying too heavily on her companionship. In a sense we became enmeshed, and I found it hard to separate from her later. It wasn't so much that I had any sort of separation anxiety (I actually liked going to friends' houses to escape the tension in my own house); it was more that I relied on her opinion and approval far too much. I had trouble making up my mind and making decisions alone. At the same time, I feared her criticism. Often she would comment on the weight of neighbors and even strangers. Though she never commented on my weight, she did try to get me to eat slimming foods and, at the suggestion of a doctor, switched me from whole milk to skim milk.

A friend of mine from high school, who developed severe anorexia after she was in college, has a mother who often makes comments about other people's weight. She has even gone so far as to offer diet tips to people she feels are in need of dropping a few pounds, even if these people haven't asked for her advice. Meanwhile her daughter is terrified of gaining weight and goes running despite the fact that she now looks skeletal. There doesn't seem to be a definite link between overly critical parents and anorexia, but I can't help but think that criticism of this nature doesn't exactly help a girl with anorexic tendencies become a self-confident, healthy adult. Many of the other girls I have met, both in my teens and as an adult, who have suffered from an eating disorder – especially anorexia – were raised in all kinds of different family situations, but the one common thread was that they did appear to be more sensitive to criticism than the average person. I certainly was.

Because I was so sensitive, people's comments went to my core, and my feelings were often hurt over trivial childhood banter. I took most comments personally instead of being able to brush them off or realize they were not to be taken seriously. (That said, many of the kids in my neighborhood could be quite cruel. I wasn't the only one who endured harsh comments, but, possibly because my peers sensed my lack of confidence, it seems that I was picked on more than most.) Once, when I was just into my teens and beginning to lose weight, my brother made a vocal observation about the large quantity of chocolate ice cream I had heaped into my bowl. I was so offended and angry at his implication that I was fat that I threw the entire glob of ice cream down the drain and stomped out of the room, a perfect example of hurting or denying myself to prove a point. (When I was in the throes of severe anorexia as an adult, my brother would confess to my mom that he would give anything if I would only eat a big bowl of ice cream.) Another time, when I was in my first year of high school, I was in the middle of preparing one of my odd little dinners, and my sister said something minor that I don't even remember – probably something about my strange eating patterns – that led to us screaming at each other. My sister and the rest of the family were aware that I was sick. I wasn't fooling anyone, even though in my mind I thought I hid my illness well. I immediately threw my plate of food against the wall and stormed out.

It took years for me to learn how to try to communicate in these types of situations rather than walk away in a huff. Even today, my tendency is to flounce, and I have to catch myself to avoid storming out and, instead, face the situation.

I was so overly sensitive that I often feared going out. As much as I loved an opportunity to play as a child, I worried about what the other kids would say or do to me. Years later, even after my self-esteem improved and I was well into my thirties, I still held on to the loner lifestyle by coming up with excuses to decline when invited almost anywhere. This kind of resistant behavior tended to push others away, and some took it personally. Though I had no problem actually being social and making friends when I was growing up, I was still withdrawn. There was gradual improvement as I got older, but in grade school, I rarely made the effort to meet new people or go out unless it was an outing that had been arranged previously by my mom. Even now there are occasional days on which I feel quite unwilling to face the outside world and would rather be by myself. It's as if I need to recharge after spending time being social.

When I was in kindergarten, I always looked forward to lunch despite the fact that I sat alone and had no classmates to hang out with at recess after lunch. Food was my companion at the time. I envied the other kids who could leave uneaten food on their tray, running out to the playground to play rather than finishing their lunch. I was oblivious to satiety but somehow had a sense that I was missing something in not being able to stop eating. I wasn't oblivious to the comments said and the tricks that the other kids played on me, though, and my feelings got overly hurt when the boys tried to lift up my skirt or called me mean names. I found these tricks hurtful and felt embarrassed by them, even though I wasn't the only target of their bad behavior. As a result, I became even more withdrawn, sticking closer to the teacher than to the other children in order to feel protected.

Convinced that I would never be the beautiful, thin social butterfly that my sister was, I accepted that I would be a fat social outcast, and I hated myself for it. I was incredibly jealous of my sister – her looks, her popularity, and her long straight hair down to her waist. My hair was wild and wavy and fell only to my shoulders. I assumed others felt the same hatred toward me that I felt toward myself. In some cases, mean comments from other kids at school or around the neighborhood confirmed the harsh view I had of myself and my self-denigrating beliefs. "Fatso" and "Lardo" were common nicknames for me growing up, so I incorporated the idea that I was unacceptable because of my weight into my self-perception. I envied my skinny sister, who was called "String Bean" or "Toothpick," nicknames that seemed far less harsh than the names I was called. Never did I think about being in a relationship or have dreams of getting married, because I believed that I was too flawed to be attractive to anyone. This belief that I was inadequate carried well into adulthood. I would eventually find that no matter how thin I got or how markedly I changed my outer appearance, I would always feel fat and unaccepted. Deep down, though, beyond the storage site of all the hurtful comments, I longed to be somebody important.

* * *

<u>Chapter 12 – Brittin Won</u>

"Every morning in Africa a gazelle wakes up. It knows it must move faster than the lion or it will not survive. Every morning a lion wakes up and it knows it must move faster than the slowest gazelle or it will starve. It doesn't matter if you are the lion or the gazelle, when the sun comes up, you better be moving." – Maurice Greene

Of the seven articles written about me after I won the Pikes Peak Ascent, these two stood out:

The Daily Camera August 1983
Young Runner Hasn't Any Big Plans – Yet
By Betsy Howard, camera staff writer

Lize Brittin wasn't too happy Sunday. Her coach didn't want her to run. The 16-year-old athlete was urged to rest after winning the Pikes Peak Ascent Saturday with a record time of 2 hours, 39 minutes and 44 seconds.

She beat last year's record of 2:41:06 set by Lynn Bjorklund of New Mexico.

The course, a steep, rocky trail starting at Manitou Springs, climbs 7,700 feet before ending 14.3 miles later at about 14,000 feet.

"We enjoy watching her run," her father said Sunday as the family relaxed in their Table Mesa home.

But he and his wife, Janine, admitted they were chewing their fingernails as they watched their daughter run because of the physical punishment such a race metes out.

The competition was stiff, too, with Lize racing in a field of 1,200 people-mostly adults. Judy McCreery, 25, of Golden, came in second place for the women, trailing Lize by four minutes. Carl Chester, 29, of Gallup, N.M., placed first among the men with a time of 2:12.54 – 24 minutes ahead of Lize.

"We don't push her, we don't try to hold her back," Wesley Brittin said.

After only 18 months of running, Lize has collected some impressive wins. She placed first in the Coors Light Challenge in Denver and the Flagstaff Run this summer. She also placed ninth in the Bolder Boulder Race May 30, and gathered numerous medals and blue ribbons in other races.

"Even if she did nothing any better, she would still have a wonderful year," her mother said.

"We're not talking about the Olympics. It's too early. She's so young. So many things can happen. We just go from race to race," her parents said, talking almost in unison.

Lize collapsed after crossing the finish line Saturday, suffering from leg cramps. But after being given oxygen, she recovered 45 minutes later.

Sunday Lize said her legs still felt a little sore and her calves were stiff, but other than that she was all right and wanted to run.

The toughest part of the course came toward the end; she recalled when she encountered the steepest part of the climb – a series of switchbacks called the Sixteen Steps.

"I kept thinking I had already passed it. There were so many switchbacks. Where I thought I was getting close to the finish I saw the sign, Sixteen Steps. I tried not to panic.

"I enjoyed it so much, no matter how tired I was."

The Denver Post Running August 1983
Record Time for Brittin at Pikes Peak Ascent

Lize Brittin made her coach look like a clairvoyant.

"She will break the Pikes Peak Ascent record in August," Roger Briggs predicted six weeks ago of his standout. "She's training well and might just be the best woman mountain runner in the world at this point."

Brittin, a junior-to-be at Fairview, this fall, didn't falter in the face of such lofty predictions.

Last Saturday, the slight youngster trudged up the 14.3-mile Pikes Peak Ascent Race with Briggs alongside her in 2 hours, 39 minutes and 44 seconds to not only win the women's overall championship but, as Briggs had boldly predicted earlier, break the course record by nearly 90 seconds and become the first female runner to break the 2:40 barrier.

In her eagerness to break the record, Brittin's early pace was too fast. That caused problems at the finish – a much slower pace and collapse at the finish line. After oxygen was administered to the determined youngster, she said the time was still several minutes slower than she had hoped for.

"She finished three or four minutes slower than she wanted to," Briggs said. "She was so cranked up at the start that we went out way too fast and I couldn't hold her back. But that's still an amazing performance by a 16-year-old girl."

Brittin's time broke the old time record of 2:41.06 set by Lynn Bjorklund of New Mexico and was nearly four minutes ahead of this year's runner-up. It was the first time she had competed in the event near Colorado Springs which features an elevation gain of nearly 8, 000 feet.

* * *

Chapter 13 – Over the Edge

"The sudden disappointment of a hope leaves a scar which the ultimate fulfillment of that hope never entirely removes." – Thomas Hardy
"If you're going through hell, keep going."
– Winston Churchill

In the aftermath of setting a new record at the Pikes Peak Ascent, I experienced both the highest high and the lowest low of my life. I read in the local papers that my coach was quoted as saying that I could have run faster if I had not started out too fast. I was convinced he was disappointed in me. What I failed to see in that same article was that he had also stated that I was quite possibly the best female mountain runner in the world at the time. Somehow I missed the positive statements and focused only on the negative or what I perceived as negative. Years later when I reread the article I was shocked that I didn't remember the incredible compliment he had given me.

After putting 110 percent of my blood, sweat and tears into something and reaching my goal, I had no idea what to do next. Where do you go and what do you do after you have reached what seemed impossible? The thought that I would have to train harder sank into me like a stone to the bottom of the sea. How could I possibly train harder than what even I was beginning to sense was already too much? To me, improvement and moving forward meant only one thing – more training. Never once did I consider training more intelligently or efficiently or in some way differently instead of simply increasing the time and effort I spent working out.

I never went to a dance when I was in high school. I stopped socializing early in my first year on the cross-country team after a late night out when a few of us who had gone to a concert were a bit off the pace in our workout the next day. Our coach told us that we needed to ask ourselves what was most important to us. For me, of course, running was at the top of the list, and my coach's statement clearly implied that if I wanted to be good runner, I should not stay out late. As a result, I further isolated myself from my friends and peers, and this in turn catalyzed an increase in the obsessive behaviors I was beginning to show – behaviors that, while unquestionably odd, I was convinced would help me become a better runner. My rituals were becoming patently bizarre and, as is typical of obsessive-compulsives, included lots of counting: my steps, the number of sips of water I drank, the number of times I entered and left a room. In addition, I was obsessed with the times of day at which I ate. I could only eat at certain times of the day despite the fact that I would wake up late at night with my stomach growling for food. I would often dream of eating or missing a workout, my two biggest fears. Like many anorexics, I grew to love cooking because it was a way to eat vicariously by serving food to others. I got all the pleasure of the food's aroma and aesthetics without the added calories. I longed to be carefree enough to indulge, but I wouldn't ever allow myself to do so. I imagined myself going out to a restaurant and ordering a normal meal or eating a big fat slice of cheesecake, knowing these scenarios were pure fantasy. I felt trapped and limited, but I experienced a tiny bit of satisfaction in knowing that I was in control of what I ate.

From the time I was young, my mom had always made home-cooked meals. They were not what I would call gourmet, but on special occasions and holidays she would go all-out and the whole family would sit down to dine. I loved watching activities in the kitchen, my mom fluttering around checking the oven temperature and stirring what was steaming in the pots on the stove. However, I reacted poorly to the tension in the air that accompanied these family get-togethers. As with most other families, we often got into arguments or slightly harsh banter during holidays and general get-togethers. I tended to assume guilt for anything that didn't go according to plan, even if it had nothing or little to do with me. For example, on one Thanksgiving my mom kept reminding everyone not to open the oven door, because the racks had been put on backward and the pies cooking inside were bound to slide straight out unless the procedure was carefully executed. My brother forgot and opened the door as I was standing there, and the hot pumpkin pie slid right out onto my feet. Of course, much chaos ensued and lots of yelling occurred. I decided the entire thing was my fault, because I had worn sandals, not the covered shoes my mom had told me to wear earlier. The pink burns on my feet and legs were minor, but my guilt ran deep. Fortunately, and to the relief of the family, the apple pie was still intact and salvaged for our dessert.

Later, when I became anorexic, I realized that Thanksgiving is an anorexic's nightmare. In fact, many holidays are. While most people spend the day giving thanks (in theory, anyway) and eating large mounds of food, I spent it trying to figure out a way to avoid the confrontation I'd face when I pushed away the food on my plate instead of eating it. For me, an excessively long run before any holiday meal often solved the problem. That way I felt less guilty about picking at the food on my plate.

Despite some trauma around meal times as a child, I grew up loving to cook. It became such an escape for me I even considered becoming a chef. Often I would make elaborate meals for others. Desserts were what I loved to make most. Our family had always been big into desserts. When I was little I remembered that dinner was just a distraction until the dessert cart rolled into view. I also remembered that with an alcoholic father, meal times were often chaotic and embarrassing, especially when eating out at restaurants. Though I did eat ice cream, I rarely allowed myself to eat outside a select rotation of predetermined meals. Instead, I would create rich, decadent desserts for contests and for other people. I won a few chocolate-baking contests and spent hours and hours perusing cookbooks and cooking magazines, imagining what it would be like to try some of the pictured dishes. I could spend the majority of the day in the kitchen, immersed in baking, and let go of some of the feelings of stress and guilt I often experienced. However, as much as I loved to cook, it was no substitute for running.

After the Pikes Peak race, with cross-country season just a month away, my coach told me to take a week off. I was heading into my junior year with hopes of winning the state meet, and I was frantic at the thought of resting, knowing that my daily routine would be disrupted. My body was tired, but my mind was overly active and I was becoming agitated. I rode my bike to ease some of the tension of complete rest and ran a little so I wouldn't forget how to run in a week. I was so thoroughly tired of this tedious lifestyle that I wished I would get hit by a car, yet even when given permission to have a break, I couldn't do it. I just wouldn't allow myself the rest I craved; I couldn't even take a full week off at the request of my coach, a man I respected and trusted at the time.

After another undefeated regular season with a few course records in place, I entered the state meet with confidence. Somewhere along the crazy route of compulsive running, I had emerged an intense competitor. Though I was meek and kind off the track, I was fiery and wild in competition, often making extremely bold moves like darting to the far outside to pass people on the track or leading races into full headwinds. My goal was not only to win but to push myself as hard as I could. Even if I was in the lead, I wouldn't allow my pace to slow. I won the state meet and soon afterward became the first Colorado girl to ever qualify for the national championship in cross-country.

The national race took place in San Diego, California. I was shocked when, at a welcome dinner and presentation featuring PattiSue Plumer as the guest speaker, I walked into a room of 31 other girls just like me. All of us had dreams of the Olympics or various other running titles. Some, like Suzy Favor (now Suzy Hamilton) did go on to reach the Olympics. I was sad at the thought that I wasn't anything special here. However, I offered myself some comfort knowing that none of these girls were the kind of mountain runner I was. The big difference with Suzy was that she seemed to be having fun. While the rest of us wore serious expressions, Suzy seemed to be able to enjoy the moment. A trip to Sea World was included as part of the pre-race activities for those of us who had qualified for nationals, and it was Suzy who led the rest of our team through the rain to see the sights. Everybody else seemed to be conserving energy before the big race, afraid to let loose, but Suzy was all for seeing the sights while she was there. I felt overly aware that I was much more a loner than many of the others, opting to stay in my hotel room instead of joining the others on the beach on the last night there, something I regret now. I wish I had been able to be more outgoing back then.

The race was intense and I fell into last place from the start. I worked my way up to the middle of the pack by passing as many girls as possible in what I considered to be a short and exceptionally fast race. I wasn't exactly happy with the 15th place finish, but I also knew that 5k was not my best distance. I didn't have the leg speed that these other girls had. Despite my middle-of-the-pack performance, I figured and hoped that with yet more training I could improve and possibly even win the next year. I paid great attention to the speech that the winner gave after her race, when she described how her strategy was to keep pushing the pace up and over the hills instead of relaxing into a slower pace at the top. I imagined how it would feel to be giving a similar speech after winning a big race. I wanted to be in her shoes.

I was heading into the winter with even more determination than before to train harder. Then, while I was on a trail run with my coach, out of the blue he dropped a bomb. He flat-out said that I was out of control. He gave me an ultimatum: Either I take a break and train according to his plan or I was off the team. That was it. There was no talk of compromise or ideas on how to help me do as he demanded; it was an either-or situation. What could I do? I was hurt and felt rejected. In addition, I was already deep into my routine and unable to retreat, so I took the "I'll show you" road and decided to train on my own.

For my coach, there came a point where he knew I was lying about my training and eating. He was forced to step back and throw his hands in the air, because there was nothing he could do. I was so headstrong that I couldn't fully appreciate his concern for my health and his worrying that I was overtraining. I was convinced he was using reverse psychology in order to motivate me to train harder when, in reality, he was trying to prevent me from getting another injury or illness. At one point the following year he agreed with my parents that I should see a counselor, which I did for several months, but before then I was determined to do things my way. I assume that my coach always had my best interests at heart, or at minimum wanted me to continue to run well, but because I was so caught up in my illness, I couldn't see that. I continually focused on random comments, not just from him but from others around me, that supported my distorted thinking. Anything that didn't fall into my warped sense of reality, I either discarded or ignored outright. That said, it was difficult to get anyone to understand that I needed help resting. The training I could handle, but I wanted someone to hold my hand through the resting phase, something most athletes are not taught. For some athletes, dealing with uncomfortable feelings that arise during between-season breaks can be the hardest part of training. I simply did not know how to do it, and nobody was willing to help me weather the storms created in my head whenever I had to rest.

I spent the next few weeks building up my mileage on an increasingly sore foot. My limp was visible, but didn't come close to stopping my training of up to 90 miles a week plus biking, one swim session and weight training. I felt so lost at the time, but was convinced that my only option was to run more. Eventually, the continual strain on my pelvis from the improper landing of my sore foot caused my pubic bone to fracture. In the middle of a run, I felt a shooting pain so intense I thought someone was stabbing me. Rather than stop, though, I hobbled the rest of the five miles back to school. I continued to train, wrapping my entire pelvis in ace bandages to lessen the severe pain. I could hardly walk down the stairs at school, yet I refused to stop running. The pain was terrible and often I would cry on my runs. Eventually, after much arguing, I allowed my parents to take me to see a doctor. The fracture was no hairline mark on the x-ray. Instead, it was a big fat line right there on my bone that was approaching a full break.

The news hit me like a freight train: If I didn't stop, I might never run again. I tried desperately to quit running, but I was a mess and couldn't make it through the day. I lost focus in school and spent most of my days crying. Even when I did attend class, I couldn't concentrate. I was terrified to eat, and when I did eat, I cried out of fear of gaining weight. Finally, my parents decided I needed help. They took me out of school and put in a mental hospital for teenagers. On my first day there, the other kids and I sat in a circle and introduced ourselves and stated why we were there. Most of the kids were experimenting with drugs, having trouble at home or stealing things, many of the very things I had been doing at age 13. When my turn came, I thought how strange the situation was and almost had to laugh, because my response seemed so silly: "My name is Lize and I can't stop running."

* * *

PART II – Black

Chapter 14 – The Comeback

"The body does not want you to do this. As you run, it tells you to stop but the mind must be strong. You always go too far for your body. You must handle the pain with strategy...It is not age; it is not diet. It is the will to succeed." – Jacqueline Gareau, 1980 Boston Marathon champion

The relationship between coach and athlete is a deep and complicated affair. It takes great skill on the part of a coach to show unconditional support to an athlete and view the athlete as a whole person, not only as an athlete. The only way this can occur is if the coach has no emotional attachment to the performance of the athlete. Focusing more on the athlete's health than on her performance is rare, but once a coach looks beyond the end result to the athlete's higher good, he can expect greatness. A coach who uniformly equates good performances with success, on the other hand, is courting disaster. Unfortunately, this is the most common type of coaching – from gymnastics to swimming – and while it may produce short-term success, it does not allow for long-term healthy careers in sports. I even heard of one runner whose coach made her get off the airplane ahead of him, because he called her performance at the Olympics an embarrassment and he no longer wanted to be associated with her. Once a coach realizes that his athlete thinks the world of him, it's very tempting to push her to her limits instead of allowing her talent to emerge slowly.

Somehow I got it into my head that there was an unspoken agreement between my coach and me that more was better. When he would tell others I couldn't run easy or always did more than I was told, I took it as a compliment, that I should continue to push the envelope when I ran. My coach called himself sensible when it came to training. He had led several teams to state victories and several individuals to state titles. I sometimes heard other runners talk about running programs that were a little on the insane side, so in comparison, our program did seem sensible. Once, while warming up for a race early in my high-school career, I met a girl from another team who was the perfect example of how not to train. She told me her coach had her run a race a week ago on Saturday, do intervals that following Monday, run a hill workout Wednesday, and do a time trial Friday, and now here she was warming up for the race on Saturday. She finished far back in the pack, behind most of the girls on our B team. She was obviously fatigued before the gun even went off. My coach was careful to keep us from doing hard workouts too close to race days, but at the same time there was an enormous amount of pressure for us to perform. In addition, ours was a high-mileage program with no complete days of rest.

I didn't find out until later that nearly every top

cross-country runner at Fairview had some sort of eating disorder. There were other girls on rival teams who also looked far too thin. Most of the girls on the team during my senior year struggled with food issues. Two girls on that very team developed severe anorexia later in life that nearly killed them both. My coach was never overly vocal about weight, but he made some definite implications that you had to be thin to win. For some reason, it seemed reasonable to him that girls standing 5'3" tall could retain health while weighing under 100 pounds. A friend of mine on the B team was told that if she lost weight, she would have a better chance of making varsity. She was 102 pounds at the time.

As I sat in the hospital with my fractured pelvis and growing fears of gaining weight as a result of not running, the thought occurred to me that I might never run again. I tried desperately to push these thoughts away, but they would continually creep back and terrorize me. Once, when I was a sophomore, my coach told his friend that inevitably when a girl runner becomes a senior, she gets fat and quits running. I was standing right there when he said it. In a grand effort to prove him wrong, I decided that if I was at risk for losing the ability to run, at least I would not gain weight.

My hospital stay was only a week long, but should have been longer. I weighed 94 pounds upon entry and by eating one meal a day and occasionally throwing up dessert. It was the first time I made myself throw up since that one awful afternoon shortly after I first became anorexic and my mom insisted I eat that hard-boiled egg. It seemed almost sensible to throw up at the time, even though I knew it couldn't be good for me. Instead of being discharged from the hospital, I left against medical advice. I walked out the door weighing 92 pounds. The head psychiatrist wanted to keep me in the hospital until I gained weight. His methods of treatment did not sit well with me. He wanted to reward each pound I gained with an increase in the amount of freedom I had. He called this "behavior modification"; I saw it as his way of trying to control me. I called my parents and told them I wanted out, that I needed out. I begged them to get me out and informed them that this was not the place for me, my peers being drug users and dropouts. Eventually, I convinced them I would continue to rest and get better on my own. I was still honing my manipulation skills despite my increasing if reluctant awareness that I was too thin.

After several days at home, I woke up one morning not feeling quite right. I stood up and started to walk out my bedroom toward the hall only to find that the room was spinning. I grabbed for the wall in an attempt to stay upright. The thud against the wall woke up my mom, and she came rushing to my side. I had nearly passed out. We both knew it was from lack of food. She coaxed me to try and eat something, and I cried as I accepted a bowl of cereal. Tears streamed down my face as I spooned the cereal into my mouth, yet at the same time I allowed the food to soothe my frayed nerves and tired body that had been crying out for nourishment for so long. I felt a little better after eating, but there remained the problem of my injury.

Sometimes in life one is lucky to have someone reach out or make a difference. Several times now, I have been so lucky. When Lisa, a good friend of mine who just happened to be my rival from another high school in Colorado, heard that I was injured, she went to talk to her coach. I suspect she was also struggling with anorexia, but it was something we never discussed. She was at least as thin as I was and had odd eating habits, like peeling long strips of the inside of a banana peel off to eat slowly before she ate the banana itself. She had heard that the inner peel of the banana contained a great deal of nutrients. The entire process was mesmerizing and took an astonishing 15 minutes to complete. It was the slowest consumption of a banana I had ever witnessed. Lisa's coach told her that without me there to compete, her chances of winning state in cross-country the next year were excellent. She told him the win wouldn't mean anything if I wasn't there, and in a gesture so unbelievably kind and caring she came to visit me, get-well card in hand. I was at home, out of the hospital, but I was still not running. I was in tears as I explained that the doctor had said I might never run again. With two full weeks of rest, my bone still ached when I walked. Lisa took my hands in her own and said not to worry. She knew I would be back and, in that moment, planted a seed of hope that would germinate in my mind until it grew into reality.

A month and a half later, eight extra pounds on my still small frame and worry suffusing my soul, I went to see my coach. I told him I was sorry for not listening to him and that I wanted to work with him again. I assured him I could lose weight, and he said that with good training the weight would take care of itself. At 100 pounds, I hardly needed to lose weight, but I had raced well the year before at a lower weight. I assumed that my coach's comment meant that with training, my weight would drop. Immediately, I felt fat. I promised I would do whatever he said. I had learned my lesson. I did not mention I had developed a little problem of occasionally binging and purging.

* * *

Chapter 15 – Tonya

"No one is immune from addiction; it afflicts people of all ages, races, classes, and professions." – Patrick J. Kennedy

It has been so long since I last binged or purged that I don't remember exactly when this was. I couldn't have been older than 29 the last time I forced myself to vomit. However, it was an addiction that lasted off and on for close to fifteen years. I always considered myself and was considered by others to be anorexic, but I struggled with bulimia from time to time as well. Oddly, I could go several months or even years without purging, only to relapse unexpectedly.

I always tried to keep my purging in check. I never purged more than a few times a week even at my worst. It seemed I was stuck in all-or-nothing habits, taking days off and binging or running and training and eating smaller amounts. My binges were never extreme. I've read about people consuming well over 4,500 calories in a single binge session, and while I could down quite a bit of food during a binge, I never approached these enormous quantities. However, I was so afraid of gaining weight that even a little too much was loads too much in my mind. This fear of fat went much deeper than being afraid of the weight itself. Becoming fat or even gaining weight represented being unaccepted. It translated into failure in my mind, and I believed that it set a person up for instant ridicule and criticism. In spite of my great fears about my body expanding, there were times when I did outright binge.

My favorite binge food was ice cream – ice cream with anything, really: cereal, peanut butter, pretzels, cookies or chocolate chips. Ice cream went down easily and also came up easily. Another food I tended to binge on was cereal. I was often afraid of getting caught throwing up, so when the need to purge would come over me, I would grab my running shoes and head to the trails. I lived a short jog from a large network of mountain trails, so it was easy to find a tree to take cover behind so I could vomit in secret. The jog leading to these secret spots I found where I could throw up would upset my stomach and this made purging easier as well. Initially it was hard to make myself throw up. I had to stick my finger down my throat, which made my eyes water and my throat burn. But over time I could just lean over, press my arm against my stomach and make nearly anything come up.

During this time it was hard to manage my diet. I ate relatively healthy foods when I wasn't binging and continued to train hard. Even though I didn't purge on a daily basis, the binge-purge cycle was nearly impossible to break. Even in the throes of it, I could go a week or two without purging, but would always eventually slip again

For many reasons, binging and purging is one of the hardest addictions to give up. The pure satisfaction of stuffing the stomach with forbidden rich foods combined with the rush of feel-good chemicals to the brain after a purge is nearly impossible to overcome. Many people binge and purge as a way to deal with stress or to avoid uncomfortable feelings. As with any addiction, It's a momentary escape from reality. Though I eventually quit the cycle, the temptation haunted me for years. It was only after the fifth year into recovery that I noticed that the temptation, even under extreme stress, was completely gone. I have met many women who have had bulimia, some of them now recovered and some still struggling. In 2005, not long after I was at a more stable weight, I was running on the trails near my house and met a woman named Tonya. I introduced myself, and we ran together for a while. I would never have guessed that this bright, inviting woman had a dark battle with an eating disorder in her past. To me she came across as a successful mother and career woman. Tonya offered me some excerpts from her past and her views on how she started to recover. I was shocked to know that during her darkest periods, she had used Ipecac to induce vomiting. It was only when she was pregnant that she was able to fully address her bulimia. As is often the case, those of us with eating disorders are more willing to stop certain behaviors in order to prevent harm to others. Eventually we learn that it's okay to be kind to ourselves, too. Before Tonya reached a healthier point in her life, she captured her despair in her journal entries, offering insight into the depression and overwhelming feelings she continually dealt with during those hard times. It's amazing to see how strong and confident she comes across now when reading the following, an account of her life in her own words and bits of her personal journal while she was struggling:

> I had an eating disorder for fifteen
> years, twenty if you count the years I
> continued to relapse. Somehow, through

it all, I finished college and graduate school, traveled abroad and kept jobs. I think the severity and length of my illness had to do with my secrecy. When I finally opened up to receiving help, I found the wrong help and fell into another addiction. Finally, in my thirties becoming a mother helped me break free of addiction and I sought therapy to piece together my broken self-esteem.

I dieted to lose weight between age 11 and 13. The pediatrician discovered my weight loss and found I was anemic so he told my mother to give me milkshakes and iron-fortified cereal. Once my mother became interested in my eating, I became secretive. When I was 12 years old and weighed 80 pounds, I wanted to lose weight without anyone noticing. I was proud of my self-control.

August 3, 1978

"Mommy keeps telling me I haven't been seeing enough of my friends lately. I don't care. Sometimes I feel trapped when I play with a friend, because I realize there probably isn't anything better to do. Today she mentioned it so I called Lynn. (She said she'd call me tomorrow.)

She couldn't play, but Francine came over and we went swimming.

Many people keep telling me "you've gained some weight there, Huh?" I haven't noticed any visible change since the Dr. told me to eat more. I don't want to look fat at all! I want to lose the weight I gained but I don't want anyone to know. If people notice I gained weight they may also notice if I lose it."

By high school, repeated diet failures led me to binging, which led to a pitiful self-esteem. I was hopeful and optimistic when I fasted, exercised, or took laxatives. I could lose 5 pounds in a week and feel wonderful, then gain it all back and feel rotten. My weight fluctuated from 115 to 145. When I first read about bulimia, I disregarded the disease. I thought purging was a great idea and I succumbed. Bulimia was different from anorexia because I completely lost control of my eating. I had a diagnosable and treatable problem, but I kept it a secret.

When I went to college I was finally free of the watchful eyes of my parents and had the freedom to totally give into my dark desires to binge and purge. When most students left for fall break my freshman year, I stayed behind in the dorm. I tried to lock myself in my room with no food in an attempt to gain control over my binging. Over the years, with unlimited food in the dining halls, I became severely bulimic. I was binging and puking twice a day and sometimes more. I felt like I had ruined my life and wished someone would save me from myself.

My first attempt to get professional help failed. I let out my secret in an eating disorders support group. I admitted that during my bulimic episodes I turned into a zombie and completely shut out reality. I would walk in a trance to various dining halls where I hoped not to be seen by anyone I knew. I found corner seats and hid embarrassing amounts of food behind the college paper. My mind was numb as I ate. Then in a panicked state, I roamed from bathroom to bathroom seeking privacy. I learned I wasn't alone in this behavior! I imagine the other girl-zombies wandered the campus every evening like I did. We respected each other's privacy since we couldn't help each other. All I learned from the support group was that Ipecac could induce vomiting.

March 3, 1987

I've discovered a miracle drug. It's so good I might die from it.

In 15 minutes the foul-tasting almondy syrup will coat the walls of my stomach, completely surrounding the partially chewed up crap that I inhaled at the co-op. And Pow, I will feel it in my throat. I'm waiting patiently, calm. I know this shit is reliable. I'll puke up my guts! I feel it coming on.

When I graduated college I moved to Colorado. I found an alcoholic and manic-depressive but very intelligent boyfriend. He was 13 years older and had five kids in another state. The relationship was sick but I finally had someone whom I could speak openly to about my dark secret. He loved me and accepted everything about me, including my bulimia. I could tell him how painful it was to have to rush off to work with hard pieces of toast up my nose from puking and he would sympathize. It even became a toast-up-the-nose loving joke between us. This intimacy was the first step in my recovery. I binged and purged less frequently. Unfortunately, I replaced my own out-of-control feelings with the chaos and abuse of a sick partner.

I met another alcoholic when I was 28 and once again, there was never a dull moment. He was handsome and charming, and full of anger from an unfair childhood. When I told him about my eating disorder, he didn't comprehend it or care. By this time it didn't matter that he didn't understand – my eating disorder wasn't so important anymore. I had new problems. I was pregnant, we were broke and he was bouncing checks to buy beer. I knew this wasn't the way my life was supposed to unfold, but my self-esteem was still the pits. While I understood that I couldn't control his alcoholic rages, I wondered how this man had so much control over me.

Like my boyfriend's love helped me break free from bulimia, my infant son helped me break free from my second neurosis – codependency. Alcohol and babies don't mix. It was a matter of survival.

I saw a therapist when I was in my early thirties. I confessed to occasional bulimic episodes in which I felt extreme maternal guilt. The therapist predicted that I'd grow out of my eating disorder. I grew into other things so that my eating disorder is a smaller part of who I am.

There was a time when I visualized myself recovered from my eating disorder: I would have a perfect, healthy, athletic body that looks good in a bikini. People would look at me and see a healthy person who has no problem with weight or body image. People would wish they had my eating habits when they'd watch me take healthy portions of all the right foods – and stop when I'm full.

I can't say recovery had too much to do with conquering food and achieving bodily health. Rather healthier eating was a consequence of regaining the parts of myself that didn't have to do with food or my body. I took pride in parenting, took a new interest in relationships, and made some accomplishments in my career. I even looked back on some of my accomplishments of the past and appreciated who I was. I had a lot of endurance! I am very sad that I wasted so much time and energy in my life, but I hope I'm a more empathetic person as a result. Bulimics experience emotional extremes. At good times I believe these extremes make me live fuller and deeper. I developed ways to release my emotions without throwing up. For one thing, I run.

Yesterday a friend lamented over a former boyfriend who always shopped and cooked for her. "It was wonderful," she said. She likes a man who cooks. I said very naturally, that I have an eating disorder and wouldn't want a man who cooked for me because I'd feel stressed out by the obligation to eat the food he made. I'm happy my boyfriend is not a cook or big into food.

I have my idiosyncrasies. For example, I won't eat doughnuts because that was a binge food and I eat cheese and crackers late at night when I want that comfort. I think the boyfriend conversation yesterday is a real statement about my recovery. Saying I have an eating disorder isn't hard for me. It's no longer a dark secret. I'm not ashamed.

Like Tonya, I have my peculiarities with food that seem to have lessened over time. However, I am aware now that these are normal. Even the most grounded human beings occasionally eat for comfort or avoid certain foods. Sometimes there is a fine line between what is considered normal and what is considered pathological behavior. With more people developing orthorexia, that line can be difficult to define. Orthorexia is a condition in which a person becomes overly focused on eating foods perceived to be pure, clean or healthy. The obsession can be taken too far and develop into a case of anorexia. For me, the answer lies in that which supports my health. If an odd behavior is interfering with my well-being, general health or happiness, it's time for a change. When I notice that I'm overly focused on food or my weight, I have to ask myself what's underneath it. What stress or emotion is at the root of causing me to obsess again? Once the feeling or emotion is addressed, it's easier to let go of the obsession.

* * *

Chapter 16 – Males and Eating Disorders

"My theory is that men are no more liberated than women." – Indira Gandhi

It's rare to think of a man when the topic of eating disorders comes up, but women are not the only ones who suffer. It's much more common for men to confess to binge-eating than to any other eating disorder, but that doesn't mean that they are immune to other eating issues. Over thirty percent of binge-eaters are male. Eating disorders in general are starting to be more recognized in men, especially gay men, who make up the majority of males with eating disorders at this point or are at least more willing to admit to having one. Many gay men already worry about prejudice and discrimination as a result of their sexual orientation, and added to this burden is the fear that their peers will judge them in terms of their weight. The term "gay fat" emerged to describe a gay man who could be seen as normal in size by most, but fat in the eyes of other gay men. Within the gay culture, there is so much pressure to be perfectly toned and lean that many men are developing an abnormal focus on their bodies and falling into disordered eating patterns. Though gay men are more likely to seek treatment than men in general, they are also developing eating disorders and body dysmorphic disorder – a condition in which people become preoccupied or obsessed with a perceived flaw in their appearance – at an alarming rate. Even though gay men are more often diagnosed with eating issues, they are not the only ones affected.

Many people agree that anorexia in men may be under-diagnosed, and there are several reasons for this. Often, physicians will not recognize the illness in a man owing simply to the false assumption that anorexia is a women's disease. According to the article "Eating Disorders in Men" by Margarita Tartakovsky, M.S., most of the diagnostic criteria for anorexia focus on women. Typically, doctors look for amenorrhea and a fear of fatness. However, men's symptoms can differ greatly from those of women. For example, while most women report a fear of getting fat or feeling fat, men might express the desire to be more muscular and still suffer from the disorder. Just as there is societal pressure for women to conform to a certain body type, the pressure on men to look a certain way is becoming more apparent as well. Lately, there has been an increase in men seeking plastic surgery such as pectoral implants, calf implants and liposuction. More often than not, men keep quiet about their struggles with food, which leads others to assume that there isn't a real problem or the problem is not severe. Obsessive exercise is common in men who suffer from anorexia. Because there are sports in which low body weight is acceptable, men who engage in these sports can rationalize that their low body weight is not an issue.

Dave Dunham, a renowned road, mountain and snowshoe racer and a recovered anorexic, admits that it's often harder for men to open up about eating disorders. He says that "there is a societal expectation for men to be tougher and not really talk about problems."

Dave's issues began after college, when his weekly mileage was increasing and his weight was decreasing. While some people exercise in order to work off calories already consumed, Dave exercised in order to give himself permission to eat. "I started running triples – three runs a day," he says. "I think this is when things really started to snowball. I didn't like running within a few hours of eating, so it became difficult to find a time to eat. Somewhere along the line, instead of eating to run, I was running to allow myself to eat. If I didn't run long enough or hard enough, I felt I didn't deserve to eat. Eventually, I got to the point where I was not eating, except for dinner. This kept the illusion that nothing was wrong. My doctor had been encouraging me to get help for a couple of years, but I kept saying that despite knowing I had a problem, I wasn't ready to do anything about it. At 5'7", I was down to 115 pounds and injured when I finally decided that it was time to get help. I bottomed out weighing less than 110 pounds and finally got into an eating disorder program." Fortunately, Dave has recovered from his illness. He no longer uses his training to feel okay about eating. To anyone struggling with an eating disorder, especially anorexia, Dave recommends throwing out the scale and eating a variety of foods.

Though reluctant to admit it, men also suffer from bulimia. When I was a young runner, I met a top mountain runner who told me years later that while he was racing and training, he had bulimia. He would not go into detail about his illness or how he eventually overcame it, but he did say that the pressure of running, racing and wanting to be thin contributed to the purging cycle.

Kevin Beck, a running coach and former sub-elite marathon runner, developed bulimia during his freshman year in college. He believed that there was such a stigma for men to admit having an eating disorder that he kept it a secret for years, though he says that he feels that he would have studiously guarded his secret even had he been female. It wasn't until he was much older that he was able to finally confess that he had a problem despite sensing those around him, especially his mother, suspected that he had issues.

Kevin admits that the illness isolated him, chiefly in a psycho-emotional sense but sometimes literally. His social life was compromised during periods of extreme binging and purging, as for all intents and purposes he was in the throes of an addictive drug at such times. For him, bulimia became a way to cope. It was an easy "solution" to always fall back on when something seemed difficult or he got overwhelmed with emotion, good or bad.

Kevin cautions anyone struggling to talk about it with someone. Even just admitting out loud that he had a problem seemed to help. It took the power out of the illness to some extent. "I wish I had said something. It's so shame-based," he says. "I wish guys would be able to talk about how they feel and express when they feel isolated and emotionally burdened. It would help dissolve internal conflict."

As far as actual symptoms, it has been reported that men and women suffer similar rates of accompanying unhappiness, anxiety, depression, self-injury and substance abuse. In addition to the bulimia, Kevin has also struggled with alcohol abuse. In general, co-existing addictions are more common in bulimics than in anorexics. Kevin attributes this to bulimics having poor impulse control, while anorexics tend to exert too much control. Samuel S. Lample, in his article "Eating Disorders: Not just a women's problem," reports that a study of 135 male eating-disorder patients revealed that across all diagnoses, 37% had a comorbid substance use problem, with alcohol abuse the most common problem (seen at a rate roughly three times that of cocaine abuse.) More specifically, Lample notes, 61% of patients with bulimia had a co-occurring substance abuse problem, and that they were three times more likely to have this problem than anorexic men.

In the same article, Lample suggests that those with bulimia show decreased prefrontal cortex brain activity but increased activity in the limbic system. This combination potentially leads to poor judgment and possible emotional problems. Writes Lample: "The strong food cravings common in those who binge eat, are linked to the brain's hedonic system, which regulates risk-taking and novelty-seeking behaviors, self-control, and pain avoidance. In short, bingeing behaviors can be seen as resulting from problems in the hedonic system around impulse control."

Despite the hope that he would one day simply outgrow the illness, Kevin still struggles with it today. Bulimia has taken its toll on him both emotionally and physically. The continual throwing up throughout the years has caused his teeth to erode, and a computerized tomography (CT) scan has shown that his brain, almost certainly as a result of alcohol, resembles that of a much older person. Kevin feels that without getting to the root of his problems, he won't be able to find better ways to cope. He can go years without binging and purging or years without drinking, only to relapse. Because Kevin understands the illness so well, he has, despite not being able to help himself, been able to offer help to others. He feels that early detection is the key to a less traumatic and more complete recovery.

* * *

Chapter 17 – My Secret

"Success is not measured by what you accomplish but by the opposition you have encountered, and the courage with which you have maintained the struggle against overwhelming odds." – Orison Swett Marden

I never told my coach about my problem with food. I kept it a secret from nearly everyone except my family, and that was only because my sister caught me throwing up in the sink after sneaking into the kitchen early one morning to binge and purge on ice cream, something I did when I was feeling either

extremely stressed out, overly tired or hungry when I
didn't want to be.

My coach agreed to take me back on the team,
and we started a training program to get me back in
shape to race. Soon I began running a little bit at a
time. My pelvis was holding up nicely. No more sharp
pains plagued me, and I could walk with a normal gait
again. I had missed my junior season of track, but
summer was approaching and I knew I could train in
the mountains with the team to get ready for my last
year of high school.

At my first big cross-country race as a senior, I
was terrified. I had established myself as the top
runner on the team again, but my confidence was
waning. There was a new girl on the running scene I
had never competed against. She was solid and fast
and swam varsity on her swim team in addition to
running both cross-country and track. Her father was
a former military man and dictated all her workouts.
On her supposed days off, she did pull-ups and extra
sets of intervals under her father's supervision. She
eventually developed severe asthma that cropped up
during and after races.

I was so nervous at the start of the race that I
could hardly breathe. It seemed that no amount of
yawning could fill my body with enough oxygen. My
legs felt heavy and tired. I tried to keep my focus away
from this new threat, but my eyes kept wandering to
her warm-up movements. Just watching her, I started
to have some self-doubt, wondering if I even wanted

to attempt to keep up with her. She looked fast.

When the gun went off, I felt overwhelmed as I found myself in the middle of the pack. The new girl had shot out to an early lead, and I could barely even see her in the distance. I tried to keep calm in the face of rising panic over perhaps not being the runner I'd once been. Soon, however, I started to reel in the runners ahead of me and settled into gradually closing the gap between the leader and myself. Toward the end of the race I was running side-by-side with her, and all of a sudden I felt it: A switch turned on and I was back. I surged, giving everything I had, and passed number one to take the lead. As I lunged for the finish, the fire that had lain dormant throughout my injury was burning fully inside me again. I crossed the line just a few seconds ahead of second place, but that was all it took for me to know this was going to be my year.

My relationship with my coach felt strained, but I did as he asked – usually. I had learned that rest was not a bad thing. I felt it was important to take days off even though my coach was a bigger fan of easy days than complete rest days. Unfortunately, my days off would sometimes lead to binges and occasional purges as well. I constantly felt fat at just around 100 pounds. My weigh-ins caused me growing anxiety, and I sensed that my coach was concerned about me getting too fat. Originally, my coach weighed me because my parents had requested that he keep an eye on my weight. Everyone seemed concerned that I might lose too much weight, but once my weight was over 100 pounds, I was convinced he was worried I would be too heavy. Whether this was in my head or not, I'm not sure, but I convinced myself that it was the case. In my mind, the occasional purges helped the weight stay off, but the reality is that purging rarely helps with weight loss. What purging offered me was some occasional and temporary relief from the pressure. What it took away from me was my sense of self. I was a more relaxed runner overall my senior year, and this unhealthy eating regime did not prevent me from having a stellar season, but I experienced tremendous guilt trying to hide my problem and worried excessively about how forcing myself to vomit would affect my health. Despite the terrible way in which I treated my body that year, I set a course record on every course I ran and won the state meet, becoming the first girl in Colorado to ever win states twice in a row. During the off-season I entered a few road races, among them an incredible 35:15 that established a new course record in the Run for the Zoo 10k in Denver. After a night of stress-related binging and purging – which in my case really meant eating what others would consider normal amounts and purging – I won the Midwestern High School Cross-Country Championships in Wisconsin and again qualified for Nationals in San Diego. I was, however, starting to feel more fatigue as the overly long season of racing dragged on. I ended up seventh at nationals and felt ready for a break. Unfortunately, track season was lying in wait, so my break was much too short.

By the time spring track season started I had already run under 11:00 for two miles indoors. There was no real indoor season for Colorado high school athletes, so my coach had me run some races at the University of Colorado all-comers meets. It was an exciting day when I broke 11:00, as my sister, who was rarely able to attend my meets due to her busy schedule at school, happened to be sitting in the stands. As our own high-school track season wore on, my general fatigue grew. I was undefeated going into the state meet, and my coach was determined to have a new state record in the two-mile for us. What should have been a walk in the park turned into a long clumsy jog around the track. My downfall actually started the day before the race; I was too fat and I knew it. I tipped the scale at a whopping 102.

Fearful of the added weight, I asked my coach if the one or two extra pounds would affect my race the next day. "It will probably slow you down," he said. I had no idea how to take that statement. I felt so guilty that I threw up what I ate that night. I was so distressed by the time the race rolled around the following day that I ended up losing sight of my goal of setting a state record. From the gun, I got out in front and just settled. I ran comfortably. The battle in my head raged on – *come on, pick it up* vs. *just finish the race and be done with it.* About three-fourths of the way through the ordeal, in mid-stride and as I was heading into the turn, I caught sight of my coach and I knew I would soon have to face him, face myself, my fatness, my apathy and my failure. I thought about Kathy Ormsby, who in the 1986 NCAA championship meet had run off the backstretch of the track two-thirds of the way through the 10,000 meters, trailing the leader by only two or three strides at the time. She ran out of the stadium without even visibly slowing and jumped off a bridge in an attempt to kill herself. Though she ended up surviving her 40-foot fall, she lost the use of her legs and is now confined to a wheelchair. It's a bitter irony, but as hard as it probably is for most to believe, Ormsby claims that she is happier now than when she was under enormous, self-imposed pressure and stuck in her obsessive training. By the time my foot hit the ground I felt detachment. "Fuck it, I'm tired," I thought. I tried everything possible to pick up the pace, but had nothing to give. My body would not respond, and my mind wavered. I finished in over 11 minutes, and when I faced the man who had led me to greatness while watching my suicide, I saw the disappointment on his face. I felt like I was an absolute failure. I had won the race, yet my perception was that I totally lost in his eyes and, as a result, in my own. I still had one last race to get through in the summer – a two-mile national cross-country race. I finished fourth in another apathetic showing. I had reached full competitive burnout at age 18.

Despite all the conflicts I had with my high-school coach, in large part I still looked up to him, even after this final race debacle. This admiration continued throughout high school and even into my college career. Shortly before I graduated from high school, I was given the chance to speak in front of the student body and faculty after winning an "outstanding athlete of the year" award. Instead of offering anything profound, I told the audience what I thought they wanted to hear and said I owed it all to my coach. While I will always appreciate the way my coach helped me achieve success in racing, today I feel sad that I was unable to acknowledge how hard I worked at the time. I also regret that I discounted the stresses my coach placed on my young shoulders. There was a part of me that felt undeserving of the attention I received, even though I had many standout moments as a runner, especially that year. This feeling likely stemmed more from my own troubled soul than from any objective lack of accomplishment.

* * *

Chapter 18 – The Stress of It All

"All glory is fleeting." – George Patton

There's no doubt that competitive running can be stressful. It is physically and mentally challenging and there's an enormous amount of pressure in any running event to give it your all. Running a race entails laying everything on the line and stepping up your game to see whether or not it's in you to go past your limitations, be they physical or mental. Any weakness is exposed for all to see, and you can be left feeling quite vulnerable out there in just a pair of running shorts and a singlet.

In contrast to countries where running is a way of life, running here in the United States is often regarded with skepticism. When I was younger, running was nowhere near as popular as it is today, and I often got strange looks from the people I ran by on the trails. In a way, this added to the pressure for me to run well, because there were so few people who considered running something people did to enjoy themselves. It made more sense to run if I could defend the activity by explaining that I was training to race, was preparing to compete, and could beat just about anyone. As a result, I was always in training, never really taking time off to regroup. I went from track in the spring to road racing and mountain racing in the summer. Then, I continued from mountain racing to cross-country in the fall, and finished out the year with a few indoor track meets and more road racing during the winter.

My high school was already a high-pressure environment. It was considered one of the top schools in the state not only in athletics but also in academics. Going to school, racing and having an eating disorder were, in a sense, like having three full-time jobs. It's no wonder my body and mind grew tired. In the summers I had one less stress by not having to worry about school, but the other two stresses were still there and growing stronger all the time.

In addition to the general stress of running, my body was exposed to an enormous amount of additional stress because of my poor running form. Unlike many other good runners, I was a "toe runner," meaning that I landed on my forefoot rather than on my midfoot. This made me injury-prone and also made it so that I had to work harder than other runners in my ability range to secure the same results. My racing style was entertaining for spectators, because I never started out in the front. Instead, I often had to come from behind and make a bold move in the middle of the race, passing the others to gain the lead. From there, it was a matter of stretching the lead as much as possible to avoid having to kick at the end. I could turn out 82-second quarter mile pace until the cows came home, ate their hay and went to sleep, but I couldn't run much faster than that if my life depended on it! My coach told me that the end of the race would always take care of itself; I knew that no matter how tired I was at the end I would give it my all to cross the finish line first. Our strategy for shorter races like the mile was to run the third lap as if it were the last and hang on to the end. Typically, the third lap of a mile race is the slowest, so it's mentally challenging to push that lap. It was crucial to get as large a lead as possible, so essentially I had to work at peak effort for the entire race.

Despite my less-than-perfect form I was obviously able to hold my own. Often, I think, it was sheer superior determination that got me to the finish line first. I had a horrible upright posture that, again, was not ideal running technique by any means. Everyone around me felt I would be a better runner if I could have had more of a forward lean. My form led me to run with a short stride, so I had to make up for it by having a quick rhythm, or turnover. Unlike the girls who had long strides and nearly perfect foot landing, a combination that naturally propelled them forward with each stride, I was forced to concentrate on pushing harder and being mentally tough. Adverse conditions were my forte. Rain, mud, wind and snow didn't scare me, and indeed were things I thought gave me an edge.

In a sense, I was the perennial underdog. Even when my name started to be recognized in the running world, my come-from-behind technique tended to excite the crowd, making it seem as if each win I racked up was unexpected. I worked on my form all through school. I practiced downhill running in order to get the feel of leaning forward more, and worked on drills to keep my knees up in front and then kicking my heels up in back, The irony was that my incorrect road racing and track form that I worked so hard to change was perfect for uphill running. I could take a more natural comfortable stride when I raced in the mountains. In addition, the soft trails were far less brutal on my body than the track or the roads. In the mountains I felt as if I could run forever. Eventually, though, even mountain running would be difficult and painful.

As much as I loved mountain running, I loved the roads and even the track as well. I just loved to run period. The stronger I became as a runner, the more I was willing to take risks and push myself, entering the elite division in major races rather than the open or junior division. Again because of my poor form, I had difficulty in road races, especially longer ones. Being a toe runner put enormous pressure on my feet. I was always at risk for stress fractures. In longer races I was constantly dealing with blisters, because instead of boasting the optimal heel-to-toe roll runners covet, I landed hard on my forefoot, causing great friction and a braking effect every time I landed.

In one 10k race, I entered the elite division and found myself running against 1984 Olympic Marathon Silver medalist Rosa Mota and other internationally recognized runners. Though I was a great warm-weather runner, having set a course record in the Diet Pepsi 5k in Denver in 97-degree heat the year before, this race would be different. By mile four, my feet were so riddled with blisters that I had to run in the middle of the road to avoid anything other than flat, even surfaces, as the slightest camber in the road caused more pressure on my feet. I took my turns extra-wide but was still in great pain with every corner. In the end, a sizable fraction of the elite field had dropped out, the stifling weather too much to bear. I finished in well under 40 minutes but also far off my anticipated time of 36 minutes. My feet suffered for days after, and I could hardly walk until the blisters started to heal.

Unfortunately, by the time I was in my later years of college, I was beginning to show signs of arthritis and stiffness. My lower back and hips were constantly sore, and no matter how hard I tried, I couldn't seem to find a comfortable stride. I would become so sore after races that easy cool-down jogs were painful. I often found myself limping the next day as well. It seemed that while I had jumped into the spotlight as a young athlete, I was slowly starting to slip off the stage. As my races became less impressive and the pain got harder to manage, I found that fans who hadn't seen my name in the paper for quite some time would often come up to me and ask the standard question: "Are you still running?"

During the times I was running well, I felt as if I were making some kind of real impact on the world, changing it or opening a door somehow. I never ran for the fame or the glory. It was always something that seemed almost beyond me, a driving force, yet there was a part of me that hoped I would do something memorable one day, something great. I thought perhaps my destiny would be reaching the Olympics or traveling to Europe to compete among the world's best mountain runners. Ultimately, no matter what event I settled on, I hoped to set a record that wouldn't be broken. "Records are made to be broken" never resonated with me – until, of course, many years later, when my own records started to fall.

In 2005, a local newspaper held a poll to determine the number-one athlete in Colorado history. I didn't hear about the poll until a friend called me and told me she saw my name in the paper. According to this poll, I was ranked 18th on the "all-time best high-school athletes ever in Colorado" list. The girl who deservedly won, Melody Fairchild, was also a runner who had broken most of my course records several years after I had graduated from high school. She attended Boulder High, naturally a rival school of Fairview. Though my school records still stand today, one girl who attended Fairview and ran cross-country years later was ranked above me on the list. Years after the fact, it's rare that people remember a standout high-school athlete, at least in a sport like cross-country. New athletes come to take the spotlight in the crowd and develop a fan base. Today, most people don't know me as a runner. At times, though, an occasional fan from the past will say, "hey, aren't you Lize Brittin, the runner?" When I hear this, it makes me cringe just a little to remember all the pain I went through during my competitive running career, but I have to smile at the thought of somebody actually remembering my hard efforts. It's touching.

Though there are some runners who may stand out on a small scale, it's uncommon for runners to be recognized to the same extent as other athletes. It's a rare that someone like Steve Prefontaine comes along, a runner so brave and strong that people remember not only the great races of his time, but the brash manner in which they were run. Frank Shorter and Grete Waitz both have had statues made of them, but unfortunately it's uncommon for distance runners to be well-remembered. Maybe with the increased interest in running in the early part of the 21st century, that will change.

* * *

Chapter 19 – Rest

"Take rest; a field that has rested gives a bountiful crop." – Ovid

When I first met Diane, I was in high school. She was someone I admired a great deal. It became known around town that I was actually following quite closely in her footsteps. Both of us were standout athletes, and not long before I set the record at the Pike's Peak Ascent, she had done the same. Our lives were nearly identical in many ways, a fact I soon discovered after she approached me in a futile attempt to prevent me from suffering the pain and discomfort of overtraining and under-eating that she herself had endured. It seemed that just as she was pulling out of her own illness, I was committed to stepping fully into mine. I felt invincible and was headstrong, and no amount of admonishment and concern on her part could dissuade me from careening toward self-destruction. However, much later, during one of the lowest points in my life, Diane was there to reach out to me yet again. This time I was ready to listen, and with her support I began a long, long journey toward improved health and increased self-awareness.

Diane began restricting her food intake at around age 14. She, like me, was facing puberty and a changing body. This caused an inner struggle, because she wanted, in effect, to keep herself from becoming a woman. Like my own father, her parents had undisguisedly wanted a boy, and she developed a lot of fear about becoming a woman. For her, food was something to control. In fact, it was one of the only things she felt she could completely control. She states:

> Perfection is the core wound of anorexia. There is an underlying fear of failure that leads most addicts to seek control through other means. In addition, as our outer world spins more out of control, the desire is to grab control of our immediate surroundings. If we keep our central world predictable, even if it's painful, it eliminates the fear of losing control. It may not be pleasant, but at

least we know where we stand, where we exist.

For Diane, a turning point occurred when, after qualifying for the Jewish Olympics, she came to the realization that she was too thin. "There were times as an athlete where I would do well, but overall, I was too depleted to consistently do well," she says. The day before the big race, she was so hungry that she ate a falafel sandwich. It didn't sit well, and Diane just blew up in the race. She had stomach cramps and felt sick. Going in as the favorite and ending up with the Bronze medal was not only a disappointment but a slap in the face. It made her look at her life and realize that she had been living in a haze of hunger, her brain fuzzy and her body weak from insufficient nutrition. It was the first time that she was able to admit the truth: that she was killing herself. She states:

> Sometimes the body, mind and spirit line up in ways we can't explain. Often this occurs when we come close to death. Somehow coming close to the veil of death allows us to have these epiphanies. At these times there is an opening that we are finally able to allow, that can ultimately lead to inviting something else into our lives. For the addict, the tendency is to want to hold onto the addiction at all costs, so it's essential to allow for the

possibility of change when it presents itself, no matter how great the fear.

As most people know, recovery from this type of mental illness begins with the admission of being ill. Diane cautions that people have to admit the problem without judging the situation; to

> become aware of where you are and from there allow for change. Don't be hard on yourself. It's important to start where you are, not from where you want to be or think you 'should' be. Act from the wisdom provided by nature, our ancestors and the world around you. The more you can flow with nature the better. I often compare myself to the weather, constantly changing and adapting. Learning to sit in the fire of whatever arises, be it fear, anger, or sadness is key to recovery. So often we want to numb out and avoid any pain, but ask yourself, 'what is this offering me?' How is this serving me? Addicts grow through the journey of addiction and through this journey we learn to discover ourselves and recognize more fully all the various parts of ourselves.

Both Diane and I are forced to live with great

regret. Knowing that we missed opportunities and chances for success due to our addiction is hard to face, yet both of us are growing and adapting well into our forties. Our addictions still tend to rule our lives, but we move more and more toward freedom. Despite our compulsive nature, we function in the world and participate.

Diane believes that once a cognitive recognition of the disorder has occurred, it's essential to take mindful action to get well. "It takes precise discipline to grow," she says. "It's a matter of allowing others in to help you take specific action, but at the same time relying on a return to the self. An important question to continually ask is, 'how does this make me feel?' As we age, we naturally move more toward self-love. This is helpful in stepping out of addiction. If the path you have chosen makes you unhappy, then the time for change has come."

In terms of anorexia, it's important to note that great fear underlies the refusal to eat. In Diane's words:

> In a sense, we become afraid of everything. We need to widen our lens of living and expand outside the box in which we have placed ourselves. It's easy to stay in the addiction, but if you look deeply at the fears around the addiction, you will find it most often comes back to fear of failure. If we don't have the excuse

of addiction, we are forced to face our authentic selves. There is no guarantee of success even if we do everything right, so if we fail we must learn to accept that part of ourselves. Addiction keeps us stuck, yet it also offers us an excuse and a false sense of security.

As Diane spoke, I tried to imagine a life free of fear and free of my compulsive and obsessive ways. We put great limitations on ourselves. Self-sabotage and tripping ourselves up have become more common than not. I often wonder what accomplishments I would have achieved if I had avoided an eating disorder. Then again, I know that I have to take what I have learned from my situation and move forward. Perhaps the most thought-provoking statement that Diane uttered when I spoke with her for this book was at the end, when she looked at me and asked point-blank: "Who would you be without this?" Thoughts of infinite possibility flooded my brain, and I too had to wonder: Who *would* I be?

* * *

Chapter 20 – New Beginnings

"How good does a female athlete have to be before we just call her an athlete?" – Author Unknown

There is a direct link between depression and fatigue. One of the main symptoms of depression is sleeping too much, or conversely, not being able to sleep, with both scenarios resulting in greater fatigue.

By the time I graduated from high school I was, in a word, beat. I was spiritually, mentally and physically exhausted. I was able to squeeze a few more road races out of myself before I was struck down with another injury, but by the time the injury hit, I was too tired to fight it. It was something more than the sore foot that had previously been an issue. That year, I had been the most highly recruited high-school athlete in all of Colorado, and I was too tired to run another step. What was worse, though, was that I didn't care.

My summer days consisted of sleeping until the late morning, reading the paper and wandering around the house, taking my bike for a spin around the block to go through the motions of training, and heading to the movie theater and out for ice cream later in the day. I was so completely exhausted that I didn't make the effort to throw up or diet even when the pounds started creeping onto my still slim body. Tensions were increasing at home with fights between my sister and me, and I wanted to get away from my dad's drinking. I was anxious to leave for college, but there was also a part of me that believed a new setting would bring an improvement in my health and training. I went to school looking to reclaim my lost motivation and to get back into running. After my recruitment trip earlier in the year, I was convinced that the coach at Brigham Young University in Provo, Utah was someone who could get me back on track and in racing form.

A few weeks before I was scheduled to pack my belongings and head to Utah for a year at BYU, I started to feel more energetic but also more panicked that I was out of shape and fat. At 108 pounds, I was a far cry from my racing weight of years and even months earlier. Despite having been on the list for a Rhodes scholarship, I opted for a full scholarship at a running program that I knew would fit my style of training. The coach at BYU was sensible and kind, and he had consistently placed his women's cross-country team in the top three at Nationals. Hard workouts on the bike didn't hurt my injured leg, so I started getting back into shape by doing intervals and longer workouts on my stationary bike. It didn't take long before I was feeling a bit more in shape despite the extra weight I was carrying.

When I arrived at my new school, I met the coach with a barrage of apologies and explanations about my new heavier figure and assured him I would shed the pounds as quickly as possible. He gave me a funny look and had me hop up on the scale. 104. He marked it on a sheet and said that I was right where I needed to be. He added that he had spoken with my parents and they all agreed that if I dropped below

100 pounds I would not be allowed to work out with the team. I was shocked. He was concerned about my health first and foremost. He didn't want any of his runners to be too thin. His motto was "train; don't strain," a distinct contrast to the "no pain, no gain" philosophy my high-school team had adopted.

For the first time in my running career, I was beginning to learn how to be healthy – at least healthier. With improved nutrition and sensible training, I grew a full inch in height, and once I was able to run again, I was back to running in top form. I was no longer the best on the team, but despite the difficult emotional transition of no longer being the "big fish," I adapted well. I won a small dual meet and placed in the top ten on a snowy course at the regional meet before nationals. It was the first time my feet had been inside a pair of racing spikes. My new coach was surprised to find out that all my high-school records had been set in either training or racing flats. I finished my first college season by placing 85th at NCAA Nationals and second at the TAC Junior Nationals. I was still fighting the food issues, but rarely did I resort to throwing up or starving myself. In addition, I was becoming a much more relaxed runner. I felt some enjoyment and excitement slowly rising out of the dark abyss that had swallowed all the fun in my life. I once again felt the desire to race.

The team was like family to me, and my coach emerged as the father figure I never had. I trusted him and did my best to follow his advice, even when my weight dropped below 100 toward the end of the first season and I had to sit out a few workouts. My new coach was firm in his decision about being healthy and strong and insisted that I wait until my weight was back above 100 pounds to train. I was forced to comply. Ultimately I knew he had my best interests at heart.

My old rival and friend Lisa and I had kept in touch by writing each other letters during our first semester at our respective schools. I had just sent her a note wishing her luck in her upcoming time trial. She was attempting to qualify for the varsity team at a university in Texas where she'd been accepted. It was my coach who broke the sad news to me that Lisa had been hit by a truck while warming up for that very time trial. She was killed instantly. Her friends and family all knew that a rare, kind soul had been lost. The girls on my own team sensed how the tragedy was affecting me and offered their support. Often, I held the thought of Lisa in my mind when I ran, knowing her running career was stopped before it fully started. At times I ran not just for myself or for the team, but for Lisa.

In terms of track season, I was recruited chiefly as a 10,000-meter runner and I wanted more than ever to shine for these new people in my life. Unfortunately, I would never run a 10,000 on the track my entire college career. In fact, I would never in my life get the chance to race that distance on a track.

After an impressive first season, I took a break from running, as suggested by my coach. The decision had been made that I would skip indoor season and concentrate on outdoor track in the spring. I sensed something was amiss in my first training run after ten days off. My knee felt funny and sore. I tried to run, but after about one or two miles, it would stiffen up and lock. I would limp back to my studio apartment, frustrated and angry at the thought of more down time. The bike didn't seem to hurt it and after so many injuries, I seriously considered starting a petition to make stationary biking an Olympic sport. When I reported back to my college coach, he immediately sent me to see the school trainers. The first thing they asked was if I had tried running through the pain. I stared blankly at them, realizing they had no clue who I was. Famous in my hometown circles for seemingly running past my body's capacity, known for running to the point of wrecking myself and idolized for never giving less than all I had, it seemed to me – probably inaccurately – that I was now being accused of being mentally weak. The thought crossed my mind that maybe they could be right, and I attempted several more times to run on the injured knee. Finally, I found a specialist who discovered some hard tissue in my knee that needed to be removed in order for me to regain my full range of motion.

It was shortly after the surgery that I questioned whether I had made the right decision coming to what was for all practical purposes an all-Mormon school when I had been raised with no religion at all. Without the running team, I had nothing holding me at BYU. I wondered if I could even find a subject to choose for a major; I had gone to school for the sole purpose of running. Studies and a social life came second to that, and all of a sudden I felt lonely and sad. I was deeply afraid that after so many serious injuries I would not become the runner I'd long dreamed of being. I wanted to reverse time and be the best, like I was when I was in high school, so I transferred back to Colorado and contacted my old coach. If anyone could help me get back in top running shape, he could. And it is probably no surprise that I was barely walking again when I returned my attention to the Pikes Peak Ascent.

* * *

Chapter 21 – Regret

"When one door closes another door opens; but we so often look so long and so regretfully upon the closed door, that we do not see the ones which open for us." – Alexander Graham Bell.

There are those who live with no regrets. I, on the other hand, envy those people who can let go and accept the choices they have made. My life is filled with regret, bad decisions, missed opportunity and unfulfilled destiny. Change is something I don't handle well, so even when the universe screams at me that something needs to change, I hang on and resist it as if my very life depends on it. It may be true that my decisions have made me who I am today, but I often sit and wonder what would have happened if I had done things differently. Often, I look not at how far I have come and how much I have overcome, but at how far I have fallen.

When I returned to Boulder, I was bombarded with round two of recruitment letters and calls. Word had leaked out that I was leaving BYU and offers of full-ride scholarships came rushing to my doorstep. I sometimes think that I might have become the runner I wanted to be had I stayed at Brigham Young University or headed to Colorado State or even some other unknown school instead of agreeing to attend the University of Colorado. Despite all the hard-to-resist full-ride offers from out-of-state schools, I declined. My choice was made and my fate was sealed. I accepted a half-scholarship at the University of Colorado. Had I known that my running career would stumble so harshly thereafter, I never would have returned to Boulder.

My first year at the University of Colorado was a redshirt year. I was allowed to work out with the team and compete as an unattached athlete, but could not score for the team. For most of the year I trained on my own. An agreement was made between my new coach and my former high-school coach that I would be following my high-school coach's workouts but would occasionally work out with the college team. This arrangement worked well. My knee had healed from the surgery and by the time summer arrived, I started training for a second attempt at the Pikes Peak Ascent. I was stronger than ever and felt great when running. I set new records in training runs and in several mountain races, including the Vail Hill Climb. Both my coach and I knew that my old record was coming down that year, and I was the one most likely to break it. I established myself as a mountain runner like none other that year, but just a few weeks before the big race, disaster struck. I ended up with Giardia, a parasite that ends up living in the intestines and eventually causes vomiting, diarrhea and cramps.

I remember the day it happened so vividly. My coach and I were out on a training run. While we were waiting at the top of one of the mountain passes for the other runners to join us, he suggested I drink some water. I was very thirsty, but hoping to share a sip of Kristen's water, as she always ran with as much equipment as she could possibly carry, including a camera, a miniature container of Kleenex and extra water for everyone. My mom had told me to never ever drink water from an outside source, even if it was at altitude, but my coach insisted it was coming from a spring and couldn't possibly be contaminated. I hesitated and then took a few small sips. Better to avoid getting dehydrated, I thought. I accidentally got a bit of sediment in my mouth and quickly spit it out.

A few weeks later, I ran a trail race in Winter Park, Colorado. Although I won, I was not feeling well at all. Later that night, my parents rushed me to the emergency room, as I was dry-heaving after having vomited everything possible from my stomach. I was so sick that all I could think of was someone putting me out of my misery. I didn't care how they did it; even a shotgun seemed an okay option. Upon my arrival, the emergency-room nurse told me I needed an intravenous line to help with re-hydration. In addition, she informed me that an injection of some drug would help ease the nausea I was experiencing. Then she roughly turned me over and plunged a needle into my backside, much too high, and hit my sciatic nerve. My leg shook and I felt an odd, almost electric sensation. My running career flashed before my eyes, but I was too sick to respond. I spent one miserable night in the hospital, wishing the nausea and pain would end, and returned home early the next morning, feeling shaky and weak but not suffering nearly as much.

Miraculously, I recovered in two short weeks by eating mostly white rice and well-cooked eggs. Knowing I had my big race coming up, I took only a few days completely off. I eased back into running with a short three-mile jog and quickly resumed my full training load. With just two weeks before the Pikes Peak race, I reclaimed my territory by unofficially becoming the first person to run the entire way up Mt. Elbert, the tallest peak in Colorado and the second-highest peak in the lower 48 states. It worried me that my right side was still sore from the shot, and my energy levels were erratic and unpredictable. In the week before the race I was looking visibly drawn, but I was committed to running as I didn't want to let my coach or myself down.

On the day of the race I woke up tired. I tried to make the best of it and warm up with a good attitude, but when the gun went off I knew I was in trouble. My legs felt like lead from the start, and I was struggling before we even hit the trail one mile into the race. By the time I got above timberline I was limping. I looked at my watch: 2:40. The record was broken and I still had a good 10 minutes to go. I crossed the finish line with blood on my shirt from excessive chafing of my nipples and a limp so severe it had caused my entire right side to go numb. In addition, my left Achilles tendon was sore from compensating. I was too tired to let my full emotions go, so I sighed and headed straight for the medical tent, where officials gave me ice for my sore tendon, a blanket to keep me warm and a congratulatory pat on the back for finishing the race.

With no time or place to shower, my friend Kristen and I headed back home. We drove the two-hour trip trying to convince ourselves that despite the bad weather and disappointing finishes, we were better off for having run the race. We made it to the top and that's what counted, at least we hoped. Trying to explain this to my coach might be another story, but for the time being, we were surprisingly satisfied. By the time I arrived home the blood and sweat on my shirt had adhered to my skin. I was exhausted and starving. I eased myself into a warm bath, fully clothed, and allowed the water to dissolve the blood sticking to my skin. I was finally able to remove my shirt and bra and wash myself fully. After dinner I was so tired I fell asleep on the carpet where I had been watching TV.

I was afraid to tell my coach about the race. Though he claimed he understood, I could hear the disappointment in his voice as I broke the news over the phone. Then, after several days of rest, something so bizarre and upsetting happened that I still have trouble comprehending it. He called me to a meeting and basically told me I was a head case and uncoachable. I didn't understand. I had just run so well that summer, setting records and winning races. I mean sure, I blew the last race, but it wasn't entirely my fault. Being in the hospital a few weeks before any event is not what I consider good preparation. I was so hurt by his words that I don't even remember what I said or how I responded. I know I did my best to stand strong and remain calm. I ran home conflicted and sad, with tears welling up in my eyes. Cross-country was just around the corner and I was on my own. I wasn't about to risk yet another injury in a program that was known to be based on too much speed work and too much mileage. As much as I wanted to stay away from overtraining, it was far too easy to get lost in the competition of who could do more when everyone around me was doing just that.

What could have been the perfect time for me to regroup and take a legitimate shot at a solid running career ended up being a pivotal point in which I instead took a nose dive into the land of inadequacy and illness.

* * *

Chapter 22 – My Mom

"A mother is someone who dreams great dreams for you, but then she lets you chase the dreams you have for yourself and loves you just the same." – Author Unknown

My mom has always been there for me. She is not only my mother but my best friend, my confidant, and my savior as well. If it weren't for her, this illness would have killed me long ago. Her take on the whole situation is a powerful one and must be heard. Too often, people assume that anorexia is caused by bad parenting, when in reality it involves far more than parent-child relationships. When I was young, I always believed that I had the best mother in the world. I felt incredibly lucky as a child to have someone I could talk to, a person who did her best to provide love and protection to all her children. In her own words, she states just how complex this disease can be:

In the movie *Gone with the Wind*, there is a scene where Scarlet stands over the ravaged garden at Tara and swears that she will never be hungry again. Her motto struck a chord with me. As a teenager during World War II, I had experienced years of severe food restrictions and like Scarlet, future survival included feeding the body properly.

And so, when Lize became anorexic I found it difficult to endure with patience that in the land of plenty she was starving herself. From my point of view her determination not to eat related to the theater of the absurd.

The breakthrough toward some understanding of this eating disorder came when I realized it was a compulsion, a compulsion very much like alcohol abuse, drug addiction and other uncontrollable activity such as overtraining or washing hands. Still the depth of the problem and a solution escaped me.

This was compounded by the fact that when Lize entered her anorexia phase, the illness was viewed and treated somewhat differently than it is now. When, all glum and solemn, my husband

and I took Lize to various facilities and psychiatrists, we were interviewed and made to confess to intimate details going back to our childhood, all of which made us feel that perhaps we had hastened the crisis and therefore were totally inadequate to participate in her recovery. Although unconvinced that experts were making progress, we accepted the verdict of no interference.

Left to ourselves and without her input we tried to figure out why she had become angry, self-willed, resentful and manipulative. We knew we had our own problems, but to just sit around feeling that some guilt was ours hardly led to a positive attitude on our part.

Fortunately, nowadays, the new approach does not seem to be so one-sided. Treatment includes some give and take. This is a huge step in the right direction because interaction helps to moderate and change what appear as irrevocably fixed ideas and inhospitable states of mind. Even as slowly as these changes take place, they are a part of recovery.

There is nothing wrong, either, in letting interaction go beyond parents into the Small Village metaphor. Anything that may help stimulate the will to get better is useful, for, in the end, the decision to get better comes from within, but it is also tied to a return of feelings that link people together. What is essential is to keep hope alive and follow through.

* * *

Chapter 23 – The Fundamental Flaw

"In a hospital they throw you out into the street before you are half cured, but in a nursing home they don't let you out till you are dead." – George Bernard Shaw

There is a fundamental flaw in the way patients are treated in eating disorders facilities. It's true that the brain needs calories in order to function properly, and only when it is functioning properly can rational decisions be made. Those who are too malnourished might need to have a feeding tube until the body is working more normally. However, there are aspects of some treatment centers that appear to be counterproductive to recovery. In her book *Feeding Anorexia: Gender and Power at a Treatment Center*, Helen Gremillion suggests that conventional treatments can actually exacerbate the problems associated with eating disorders. "The patients in the program I studied are required to have an exact calorie count every day. There is also detailed attention to even very small weight gains and losses," Gremillion reports. "Of course, any treatment program must devise ways to encourage eating and weight gain, but I argue that such careful attention to the numbers plays right into anorexia's hands. The focus of the treatment takes on a life of its own to the extent that it ends up reinforcing the problem." She adds, "Young women today are expected to carefully monitor their consumption of food, and people who struggle with anorexia are caught up in this ideal with particular intensity. Treatment programs that don't recognize this cultural pressure can contribute to it when they require patients to monitor their body size very carefully," She suggests that "The goal of weight gain vs. weight loss in treatment pales in comparison to practices of self-control and self-surveillance that both anorexia and mainstream treatments for it require."

Though it can take months and even years before recovery takes place, most insurance companies only cover approximately six weeks of hospitalization for an eating disorder. The 2006 documentary *Thin* tracked several women with eating disorders during their stay in a treatment facility. It is one of the most deeply disturbing movies I have seen, not just because it hits close to home but because it gives an honest look into the suffering that victims of an eating disorder must endure. In one heartbreaking scene, a woman is forced to leave treatment when her insurance runs out. In another, a woman's mother begs for the administration to let her daughter stay after the decision was made to kick her out for breaking hospital rules. Rather than addressing the issue and realizing that rebellion is a common trait of many anorexics, the woman is forced to leave before she feels ready. It becomes clear in the movie that an "us vs. them" attitude is rampant at the hospital from the way the women talk about the administration and purposely break rules. Compliance is the best way out of treatment, and many women become model patients with the thought in mind that they can return to anorexic behavior once they get out.

The difficulty that treatment facilities face is that gaining weight does not cure anorexia. An August 2005 study in the *Journal of Clinical Nutrition* by Robyn Sysko even showed that improvements in both psychological symptoms and weight did not necessarily lead to a similar improvement in eating habits. The study reported the following:

The researchers fed 12 hospitalized women with anorexia and 12 women without eating disorders the same number of calories at breakfast followed by an unrestricted-calorie test meal at lunch. The test meal consisted of a large strawberry yogurt shake. Study participants were told to drink as much or as little as they liked. The anorexic patients were given the test both early in their hospital stay and later, after they had gained back a good deal of weight. The non-anorexic study participants ended up drinking about half of their shakes, taking in approximately 500 calories. Early in treatment the anorexic patients took in about 145 calories at the test meal, and later in treatment they took in 240 – still less than half of that eaten by the women without anorexia nervosa.

The study concluded that those with anorexia, left unsupervised, were more likely to eat less at mealtimes.

It appears that hospitalization does not always lead to recovery from the illness. Indeed, many hospital treatment programs seem to have an almost backward approach to treatment. Of course there is a need to address food issues, but what is questionable about the typical course of action is taking the control completely away from patients when they walk through the doors. This immediately puts an air of distrust in the treatment itself. In addition, by controlling patients' food intake, the focus is still primarily on the food, only now someone else is establishing the rules. These rules may be healthier than what was done before, but they are still rules nonetheless. Forcing patients to follow a strict meal plan leads to a distrust of one's own body, and relying too much on a food plan doesn't allow for natural changes in life, be it hormonal or physical, that cause the body to naturally need more or fewer calories or different nutrients at various times.

When my friend Laura was in the hospital being

treated for anorexia, she was not allowed to mix her food. For example, if she was given granola and yogurt, she had to eat the two separately. She was also made to eat at regular times during the day and had to consume absolutely everything she was given. In many cases the food is actually weighed out and exact amounts are measured.

Laura relapsed relatively quickly after her release and is at the point where those around her, as of this writing, are worried for her life. The last time I saw her, in 2011, she was out shuffling through a jog, looking like she was living in a country overcome with famine. Her mother cried when we discussed her condition. After meeting with Laura for an interview for this book, I felt compelled to send her an email expressing my concern. Unfortunately, and I know this from experience, it's rare that an outside voice can change the course of a determined anorexic. However, I feel it's essential to keep trying or at least not give up hope.

Another hurdle with recovery comes through the pressures of society and the flawed messages sent to us all. In magazines, it's not uncommon to find the image of a frightfully thin model on one page followed by a fast food ad on the next, followed by a diet cola ad on the next. It's very confusing. Both anorexia and obesity are reaching epidemic levels. The diet industry is capitalizing on selling the public foods that are energetically dead and devoid of essential nutrients with claims that these products will help a person lose weight. A study by Sharon Fowler in 2005 at the University of Texas suggested that diet soda increases the risk of obesity by 37.5%, while drinking the same amount of regular soda increased the risk of obesity slightly less at 30%. In the 2004 movie *Supersize Me* it was shown that children are bombarded by messages to eat fast food, and that this very food, if eaten regularly, can lead to illness and obesity. The messages are either subtle but continual, or blatant. Obesity is reached one Big Mac at a time, one missed workout that leads to more missed workouts, and the cure does not come in a bottle. What needs to be addressed is basic psychological and physical health together. These conflicting messages we receive from the media lead to an unhealthy attitude about what is important in life, which is a healthy lifestyle, feeling good and being happy, not being rail-thin or conversely eating as much as possible.

Another problem with getting well in this society is that it is nearly impossible to get any kind of financial assistance for eating-disordered patients. Though I was at one time eighty pounds, jaundiced and having seizures, I was not considered disabled enough to receive any government assistance. A lady I knew with bipolar disorder, on the other hand, was given assistance. In addition, there are those who are able to receive aid when they are not managing their lives well. It's a very subjective decision to reward one person over another monetary assistance, and I'm not sure what leads to these outcomes. At the time, when I was so very ill, it felt like the decision was reached by the toss of a coin or whether or not the intake forms were received by someone who had just had a good breakfast or not. It seems ridiculous to me that someone so close to death would be denied help, yet someone else whose survival does not depend on assistance may be offered help.

Although psychiatry claims it takes approximately one month to change a behavior, this is not always so with addiction. Stopping smoking for a month, for example, does not necessarily mean the smoker will never touch another cigarette. Recovery takes more than just behavioral modification. This can help a great deal, but what needs to be addressed goes far deeper. We as a society need to recognize the triggers that lead to disordered behavior, so that we can better deal with the issues. It's essential to consider the inner working of the person, which may or may not correspond to standard theories on recovery. When it comes to treatment and recovery, each person must be dealt with separately. A return to the self should be emphasized, so that each patient can assist in her or his own wellness.

* * *

Chapter 24 – It's All in Your Head

"The turning point in the process of growing up is when you discover the core of strength within you that survives all hurt." – Max Lerner

Freud did nothing but further the plight of women's rights. His theory of women and hysteria blatantly discounts the possible physical and emotional reactions to stress. When a woman goes to the doctor's office, she is often discounted before she even announces her symptoms. If her symptoms are not detectable using a general blood test, it is often assumed she is faking them to get attention. If a doctor sees a patient with an anorexic past, the assumption is sometimes made before any tests are even run that the illness is not real. Even in cases where there is real illness, it is assumed that she brought it on herself, and getting proper treatment can be quite a challenge.

My last few years of college were a bit of a blur. After so many intense years of training on too few calories, my body was starting to tire. My immune system was shot, and I was continually without energy. Each day consisted of sleeping as late as possible, dragging myself to class, crawling to the library for an hour-long nap before practice, training and then heading straight home for dinner and more sleep. Though I longed to run, I no longer had the energy. With swollen glands and pallor that nobody could deny, I approached the head coach on one of our scheduled hard days. He told me to get through as many intervals as I could, so I continued to train through my illnesses as they got progressively worse. Over the course of one six-month period, I wandered from doctor to doctor complaining of great fatigue and a low-grade fever. Each time, I was given a routine blood test that showed I was on the low end of normal for everything. Several times, doctors suggested this sickness was in my head, and I slowly started to believe that perhaps I was, indeed, losing my mind and manifesting phantom illnesses. However, since the symptoms felt so real to me, I did not give up hope that a doctor might eventually find out what was wrong with me physically. Eventually, I saw an endocrinologist who found that my thyroid-hormone levels were very low. In fact, the gland didn't seem to be functioning well at all, even when stimulated. I was officially diagnosed with hypothyroidism.

It was then that my doctor suggested I see a nutritionist. He felt that a better diet would help me feel better more quickly as I got used to the thyroid medication. After a few visits, the nutritionist asked me point-blank if I was over my anorexia. I told her that while my body weight was up somewhat, it was still an issue in my head. She thought it would be best if I could stay in a hospital specifically for eating disorders. My obsessive-compulsive lifestyle was all too obvious no matter how hard I tried to hide it. Exercise still took priority over everything, and I was holding the reins so tightly on my food intake that I constantly felt guilty for any crumb I consumed outside of what I felt I "should" eat. I had already read a great deal on recovering from eating disorders. Geneen Roth's books were an inspiration to me, and I was trying to determine when I was hungry and also when I was full. The problem, it seemed to me, was that I didn't always eat when I was hungry or stop when I was full. After much consideration, I entered the six-week eating-disorders treatment center with the full intention of breaking free from my addiction. I knew that what I was doing wasn't working, so I trusted that someone else might have some answers.

The first day in the hospital was miserable. I was told I couldn't work out for the first three days. In addition, I had to eat everything on my plate at each meal. The other girls and I were fed three meals a day with an optional snack that nobody ever even considered consuming, except one girl, who had checked herself in for compulsive overeating. My metabolism started to kick in when I began to eat normally. The first two days I was starving. All of a sudden I worried that they weren't going to feed me enough! The other girls watched me go through the struggles that they had recently endured. There was one girl who weighed 60 pounds when she first came in. She had edema so badly that her doctors made her wear stockings to help the circulation in her legs. When she first started to eat, her body didn't know how to handle the food. She had to be watched 24 hours a day until her body could adjust. All of us were constipated, anxious, depressed and had digestive troubles. A single Ex-Lax tablet was part of every girl's morning routine, except those who had abused laxatives outside the hospital. Normal elimination was something that would take many weeks to achieve. By the third day, my body began to adjust to the eating pattern and I was full. I ate three-quarters of my lunch and put my fork down. The other patients eyed me with a "this isn't going to fly" look. At the end of the meal the counselors reminded me that I had to eat everything. "Yeah, but I'm full," I replied. They told me I didn't know yet what my body needed and that, for now, I had to eat what I was given. I could see that this was the "Goddamn egg" scenario with my mom all over again, only there was no way for me to throw up what I didn't want to eat. I had to let go of my control, so I cried. I was angry as I forced the food down. It did not seem at all healthy, but I was also on a mission to become a model patient, so did as I was told – with one exception: I didn't drink all of my milk. It was in a carton, so I could easily hide the fact that I left some every night. Somehow I had to retain at least some sense of control... in my mind, anyway.

Most of my time at the hospital was spent journaling or going to meetings. The days were very structured, with exercises and various kinds of therapy and lectures to attend, some mandatory and some optional. One exercise in which everyone had to participate was drawing a life-sized image of ourselves on paper. We all drew an image much larger than our actual size. It was clear we were all struggling with body-image issues, and nearly everyone was plagued with fears of failure and of getting fat. "I feel fat" filled page after page of the plain notebook paper I used as my hospital journal. The other girls and I shared "food feelings" after every meal, and again, "I feel fat" was my typical response. Feeling fat, I discovered later, was a blanket statement for any discomfort in my life, and while it's true that I did see myself much heavier that my actual body size, I never resolved how to convert my feeling "fat" into the underlying emotion. What was worse was that I had no idea how to handle the real emotions once I discovered them, especially anger.

Often, I felt alone in the hospital. Though the other girls there were all going through something similar to what I was, it wasn't until Julia stepped onto the floor of the unit that I felt that there was someone I could relate to there. Eventually, we became friends. Julia was admitted to the hospital by her parents because she was bulimic. Right away I could see that she wasn't exactly invested in her recovery. She had friends on the outside sneak Zingers into her room when they would visit so she could binge and purge. She was younger, but we became quite close. Both of us had a hard time with the long hours of the day, so we tried to make the best of it. We even tried to make it fun. In fact, on April Fool's Day we tried desperately to come up with a way to order 12 large pizzas. We were convinced it would be hilarious to see some guy deliver a large number of pizzas to a room full of anorexic girls. Although we never did find a way to accomplish the prank, we had a good time coming up with the idea. She and another frail woman I met, Sarah, were incredibly supportive, and the three of us quickly formed a strong bond.

When Sarah first arrived, she was gaunt and exceptionally tiny. Her every movement was hesitant, yet she carried herself with elegance and grace. She looked far younger than her 30 years and had no problem associating with girls much younger. It was easy to see that she was terrified of eating. At her first group dinner, we were all served an unfortunate "oven fried" chili rellenos that looked like a mess of fattening cheese rolled into a greasy crumb coating. It was enough to intimidate even the most normal of eaters, and Sarah nearly broke down in tears just looking at the plate. I tried to reassure her that it got better, that she should just do the best she could to attempt to eat it. She was only able to manage a few bites before she completely broke down and confessed that her obsessive-compulsive disorder caused her to visualize things in her food. Not only was she dealing with the trauma of having the control taken away from her, she was dealing with phantom bugs running around on her already intimidating dinner!

As I got to know the girls on the unit better, we became like family. And just as every family has issues, we developed our own. There was one girl who was bulimic whom I found very intimidating. She never hid her anger and often blew up at a moment's notice. When she stormed out of her therapy session in tears one day just before lunch, my first instinct was to go comfort her. Instead, I worried that she would lash out at me. I worried too that the counselors would not allow me to hold up the group when we were scheduled for lunch. Meal times were often anticipated, feared or dreaded, but they were always held at exactly the same time each day. None of us dared alter the strict schedule, so I followed the rest of the girls to the lunchroom, all the while sensing this girl's increasing anger and sadness. She didn't utter a word the whole time, but at the end of the meal she let us all have it, saying how shocked she was that not one of us came up to her in her time of need. I countered with the fact that her unpredictable nature did not make her very approachable, but deep down I knew she was hurt. I hated that I let my fear stop me from doing what I knew was right. We worked it out by simultaneously apologizing, and we eventually ended up as friends. I learned how important it is to follow one's heart and go with initial instincts. I also found that ultimately, these girls were some of the most supportive, kind and caring people I had ever met. We all shared our weaknesses, fears and hard pasts with each other.

In one exercise we did as a group, all of the girls were supposed to go around in a circle and say one body part we liked on ourselves. I frantically went from head to toe eliminating every part for various reasons: too fat, too ugly, too oddly shaped, etc.

When it came to be my turn, I was at a loss; I stared blankly and couldn't bring myself to say anything. I looked from girl to girl and tried to utter something, but I just couldn't lie. The silence became uncomfortable. Sarah blurted out, "Her eyes." Oh, thank God, my eyes! Yes, that I could accept. "My eyes," I agreed. It was the one and only body part I didn't despise.

Probably the most important thing I took with me from my stay at the hospital was how to be honest. I had always tried to be fairly up-front with everyone around me. I never wanted conflict or to hurt anyone's feelings, so I occasionally let slide a few minor white lies, but in general I considered myself an honest person. When one of the nurses gave a lecture on honesty and how it plays a role in addiction, she asked us all how honest we were with ourselves. I realized that not only did I occasionally blur the lines of truth when it came to explaining my eating habits and overtraining to others, but for a long time I had also been fooling even myself. Anorexia is a sly illness. It continually tries to creep its way back into one's life. "Oh, it's okay to skip a meal or cut back here and there," it says, when in reality it's a step closer to letting the dangerous malady back inside to consume the mind. I realized that being truthful with myself was going to be the most important factor in getting better.

When I left the hospital after my six-week-long stay, I was feeling more confident. I had a new diet plan and had already tested eating out at restaurants. Sarah and I kept in touch for many years after our hospital days. She continued to be plagued by compulsive behavior, but became much healthier and didn't have to open 12 yogurts to find one she could eat. Julia and I hugged before I left. Something told me I would see her again soon. I was sad when, a few months later, we both relapsed and ended up back on the same unit. Julia had been rushed to the emergency room after fainting from not eating enough, and I was admitted after slitting my wrists and downing half a bottle of aspirin. We were both on large amounts of Prozac prescribed by our psychiatrist at the time. Seeing Julia there, hooked to an IV, made me wonder if it was possible to beat anorexia. I questioned whether I would ever recover or get better. I certainly didn't think it could possibly get any worse.

* * *

Chapter 25 – Lost

"It is not the strongest of the species that survives, nor the most intelligent that survives. It is the one that is the most adaptable to change."
– Charles Darwin

When I was little I was terrified of death. My dad, being the hard-core scientist that he was, told me that when you die, that's it. At the moment of physical death, humans simply cease to exist. At age four, I tried not only to imagine what nothing was like, but also to imagine an eternity of nothing. Often I would become so scared I would turn pale and people around me thought I was sick. My tiny brain just could not wrap itself around the concept of either eternity or nothingness, so death became my biggest fear, along with spiders, which for some reason I tried to like in order to please my dad, who liked the creepy little buggers. However, from puberty on, gaining weight became my biggest fear. Oddly enough there is a homeopathic remedy that deals with all three fears – fear of gaining weight, fear of death and fear of spiders – that is made from the tarantula spider. I tried it once and did notice a very slight easing in all three of these fears, but question whether the improvement was due to the work I was already doing on myself or the remedy.

When I was a teenager, everyone knew I was anorexic. It was obvious. When I first got out of the eating-disorder treatment center in my twenties, though, I fell somewhere between "normal" and sick. I appeared normal, but was still terrified of gaining weight and was overly focused on what I ate. When I started to fall off my meal plan and became too tired to work out, the pounds naturally started creeping on. I became depressed. My psychiatrist upped my Prozac levels, but this only seemed to make me more discontent. In fact, I started to feel completely unlike myself. I even noticed that my handwriting was changing. I was agitated while clinically depressed and my thyroid was still not functioning as it should. In a frantic move, I cut my tongue with a razor blade in horizontal lines, hoping this would somehow get me to eat less. Knowing it was a completely irrational act did not stop me from mutilating my tongue, and yet even that didn't help me eat less. I ate despite the discomfort in my mouth. Nothing felt right. I was so miserable that I wanted out. I didn't care how my pain ended; I just wanted it to end. Since I couldn't see a way to get better, I tried to slit my left wrist. The fight between my fear of death and my fear of living in my current state was raging in my mind. I had no idea which fate was worse – nothingness or fatness. In addition, I didn't know if I had it in me to off myself, but I decided I was going to try.

I knew the correct way to cut my wrists – along the arteries, not across them. When I tried, though, I got too scared. The blood was so vivid and red, it made me falter. I didn't want to see the life drain out of me, so I searched for another option after bandaging my wrist. Swallowing pills seemed a much calmer way to go, so I started swallowing aspirin, one after another, until I lost count. With a handful down, I felt a surge of calmness. It was at that moment I wavered. I wasn't convinced I wanted to die after all, so I told my sister and was taken to the hospital, where they re-bandaged my wrist and gave me charcoal for the toxic level of aspirin in my body. After vomiting up everything in my stomach, I was admitted to the eating disorders unit again and stayed just a few days to stabilize.

I spent most of my time alone the second time at the hospital. I refused to go to lectures or groups and was there only to be supervised while I was slowly tapered off Prozac. Going off the drug too quickly can sometimes cause debilitating withdrawal symptoms. Julia seemed far gone and for some unknown reason was having severe nose bleeds. She was bedridden, hooked to her IV and extremely pale. The doctors were threatening to put a feeding tube in her nose if she didn't eat something soon. She was transferred to the medical hospital after she passed out for a second time. I assume the tube went in. Although I made great efforts to stay in touch with her afterward, my letters and messages went unanswered. Even her family would not tell me whether she made it out alive. I can only hope Julia found the strength and courage to survive. After being discharged, I vowed that if I ever attempted suicide again, it wouldn't be a half-assed job. I was embarrassed at what I had done and could hardly face even my closest relatives.

Oddly enough, getting off Prozac was the best thing that could have happened. At one point, it was thought that decreased serotonin levels in the brain led to anorexia. Today, research points to the possibility that it's actually too much serotonin that may contribute to anorexia. In a sense, some feel that anorexics are "self-medicating" by unconsciously restricting foods that would be broken down into the precursors of serotonin.

After stopping the Prozac, I experienced a return to myself. My weight dropped slightly to just around 100 pounds, and I felt more in control. The depression also seemed to lift.

Unfortunately, the next few years would be a roller coaster of more illnesses and injuries. Over the course of a single year, I was diagnosed with several viruses, mono, ulcers, walking pneumonia, an absorption problem, and tonsillitis. I was basically sick every two weeks. I did my best to train and go to school despite chronic fatigue and continual down time. After one doctor told me I had asthma, I used an inhaler for a while. I ran 36:36 at a 10k race in California wondering if the humid weather was affecting my breathing. It turned out I was misdiagnosed and what the doctor originally thought was asthma showed up on an x-ray a month later as pneumonia. When I went to an ear, nose and throat specialist about yet another sore throat, he could see the emotional strain all this illness was having on my basic outlook on life and decided to take out my tonsils. Even though the tonsillectomy did help my health improve, my college career was coming to a close before I could get fully back on my feet. Despite running varsity for the cross-country team my last year, I felt off and wondered if my entire running career was ending before its time.

Shortly before college graduation, I started

training with a local coach. The relationship was short-lived, because after I ran 38 minutes for 10k on the roads, he claimed that I was washed up and needed to take at least a year off. He refused to coach me anymore. This was another example of a coach not willing to help an athlete through what some consider the toughest time for a runner – a necessary rest period. Back then, most coaches gave the impression that they only wanted to deal with an athlete if that person was already running well. There was no offer to guide me through what I knew would be an uncomfortable situation if I even could attempt the down time. Despite some improvement in my general health, I felt burned out. Sadly, I had no idea how to live life apart from running. The thought of not running was terrifying. I didn't know how to eat if I didn't run. I had no idea how to deal with life if I didn't run, and I had developed a compulsive routine that I clung to with everything I had. Winning started to be less meaningful than my routine, but I wanted so badly to be back on top. I just couldn't figure out how to stop being so compulsive with my exercise. So, instead of quitting, I decided to up my distance from the 10k to the 15k. It was a good distance for me. I even won a little prize money. In the past I had not been allowed to accept cash or prizes, because I was trying to keep my amateur status, both for a possible Olympic bid and for racing in college. This time I could accept it. The rules have changed now, and young athletes are often able to put cash earnings in a trust fund.

Somehow during this time I was able to have an on-again-off-again relationship with a runner from the East Coast who had moved to Colorado to attend school. The relationship was more off than on again for two years. I did have periods where my health was good and I felt emotionally stable, but my lows were extreme and even I didn't expect anyone could handle being around me. There was no doubt that, in addition to all the physical ailments, I was still struggling with depression. Whether it was my fluctuating moods that caused it or simply that he found someone else, we split up for good shortly before I graduated from college.

During one of my extreme down periods, I checked myself into a hospital for depression. Unlike the strict rules at the eating disorders unit, the depression unit was casual and meetings were optional. After attending a few, my roommate and I decided the meetings were not useful, so we holed ourselves up in our room instead. We snuggled in our beds and took turns reading (in our most melodramatic voices) excerpts from romance novels that caused us to burst out laughing. Though thoroughly depressed, we felt better when we could talk and laugh, and the two of us formed a close bond.

It turned out one of the girls on the unit was bulimic. She had previously tried to kill herself by overdosing on sleeping pills and anything else she could find in her cupboards. After three days she woke up dehydrated and dizzy. Unaware of how many days she had been out, she called an ambulance and was rushed to the hospital. She was admitted to the depression unit shortly thereafter. I was shocked that nobody went looking for her in the three days when she was passed out and nearly dying! It was worrisome to me that none of her friends were concerned when she had not returned calls or showed up at work. She explained this away by saying that her schedule had always been flexible, and people probably just figured she was taking some time off. I wondered whether anyone would notice if I were to go missing for that long. The two of us remained friends for a few years after our release. Eventually she got married and had children. It took becoming pregnant for her to stop purging, but she did it.

Right after I got out of the hospital I took a job as a nanny for two children in middle school, a boy and his younger sister. I helped them with homework and drove them to various activities. They picked up on my unusual eating habits right away, and I had to let on that I had issues. I worried about the girl because she was so thin. I couldn't stand the thought of seeing this beautiful child go through what I had gone through. I allowed her to eat anything, even the most sugary snacks, because otherwise she would hardly eat at all. I cooked pasta and pancakes whenever she wanted and offered to make runs to the store so she could pick out a snack. We talked openly about eating issues and I sensed she might be struggling. Years later I found out she did have a serious bout with anorexia while she was in high school. At the time I suspected she had tendencies toward anorexia, I was unable to protect her from eventually falling into this kind of illness. As much as I wish I could have changed her fate, nobody could have done so. Her future was in her own hands.

While I was working as a nanny I did a photo shoot with a modeling agency, thinking that it might help my self-confidence to step into a career in fashion. I knew that agencies took all sorts of people for various kinds of work. Incredibly, the photographer told me that if I wanted to make it as a model, I would have to put on a few pounds. I was shocked. I had always assumed that models were supposed to be thin, and I couldn't accept that I was too thin. Nothing ever came of my modeling attempt. After a few rejections, one for having "skin that's not flawed enough" – they wanted to try a product and needed a "before" shot – I decided I didn't have the energy to make the long drives to modeling calls in Denver anymore. I also knew that any kind of rejection, no matter how carefully worded or cushioned, was not helping my self-esteem.

A few years of working as a nanny had passed and I realized I was beginning to lose myself. I was growing tired of my life and the rut in which I found myself. I had a degree in psychology after studying behavioral neuroscience (which my dad claimed was not a "real" science), but I decided not to attempt grad school, even after doing reasonably well on the GRE.

Obviously there was no pleasing my dad academically if I couldn't be a female version of Einstein, and that was unlikely to happen with the physics gene having bypassed me.

It was starting to look like I had nothing left in my life. The more depressed I became, the more weight I lost. It was subtle at first, but I was down to 95 pounds before I knew it. I was struggling with my identity, and no longer able to define myself as an elite athlete. The transition from elite athlete to normal person was incredibly difficult. It was almost like experiencing a death in the family. I wasn't ready or able to say goodbye to a sport that had been such an important part of my life, but I knew I was no longer the athlete that I once was. I thought saying goodbye was a must.

I felt that I needed a radical change after I graduated from college, so I looked into joining the Peace Corps. Unfortunately, I was diagnosed with diabetes insipidus, a rare form of diabetes that I learned later was related to my anorexia. My pituitary was shutting down and I was no longer able to regulate the water balance in my own body. I was constantly thirsty. In addition, I was constantly running to the bathroom to pee. It seemed to be a catch-22 – if I drank amounts of fluid that didn't force me to void constantly, I'd become dehydrated. Since I was unable to join the Peace Corps, I took a job as a teacher at a preschool. My weight continued to drop.

One day I had a fleeting thought about what it

would be like to be less than 90 pounds. It was just a blip of a thought, but I started to actively pursue it. I was so completely tired of my compulsive training and eating habits that I could not for the life of me see a way out of them, and I decided to give it all up cold turkey. And just like that, I quit running. I was still determined not to gain weight, so I came up with a way of estimating calories and allowed myself just over 1,000 calories a day. Occasionally I would binge and sometimes resort to purging, something I thought I would never do again after I had stopped doing it in college.

My complete abstinence from exercise didn't last long. I started some biking and walking, but I did less the weaker I became. I was on a path of total and complete apathy. I was living in limbo between life and death, too afraid to take a stand either way, so I lingered.

My sickness was so overwhelming that it didn't even seem all that odd to me to be living back home with my parents at the time. I couldn't imagine living the life of a normal woman. I no longer even felt human. The reality was that I was a ghost of my former self, slowly disengaging from the world. Relationships were out of the question. Socializing was not on my mind, and I no longer had any kind of real goals. I refused to go out to eat with anyone, and my life seemed secretive and lonely. So much of my mind was consumed with what and how much I ate. While other women my age were planning their lives, with or without partners, or establishing themselves in their lives, I was fading.

For over three years my weight hovered between 80 and 85 pounds. I was living breath to breath, often wondering if that next breath would come. I quit working at the school and took a job cleaning houses twice a week. As I was living at my parents' house, my mom started a routine of morning and nightly checks to make sure I was still breathing. Many times she expected to wake up to her daughter having died in her sleep. As much as she wanted to help and dreamed of seeing me get well, there was nothing she could do for me.

* * *

Chapter 26 – Fear

"What is life? It is the flash of a firefly in the night. It is the breath of a buffalo in the wintertime. It is the little shadow which runs across the grass and loses itself in the sunset." – Crowfoot, Blackfoot warrior and orator

Sometimes a person can get so caught up in a certain identity that he forgets who he really is. There are others who are more spiritually evolved who have an innate knowledge that who they are is not based on how much they make or what car they drive or even how fast they run. Self-acceptance is not often taught in this country. Celebrating yourself just because you exist is something I wish I had learned. Instead, it's something I'm still trying to grasp.

By the time I reached 80 pounds, I had become so good at deception that I was even fooling myself. I was still honest as far as admitting I had eating issues, but I was so lost in the disease I could no longer decipher what was good for me and what was not. I was giving myself enemas daily, pretending it was helping rid my body of "toxins," something I was told by a "healer." Looking back, I realize that these enemas simply made me feel thinner, nothing more. That was the reason I continued to do them, not for any possible health benefit. My new identity was entirely wrapped up in my illness, and there was an incredible amount of fear around all of my actions. I was outright terrified of gaining weight at that point. I convinced myself and tried to convince others that the diabetes and other symptoms of anorexia were actually what caused the anorexia to become so severe, when in reality it was the other way around. The anorexia was causing all the other issues. It's an odd thing; on some level I knew I wasn't fooling anyone, yet on another level I actually believed my twisted explanations. I had lost sight of how thin I actually was. On the other hand, I was fully aware I was sick. People on the streets stopped and stared, mouths fell open when I walked by and looks of concern and fear surrounded me. Occasionally, someone would actually say something about how thin I was, but it was rare, not like when I was heavy as a child when everyone insisted on offering an opinion. Somehow being ridiculed for being fat is much more acceptable than being singled out for being thin, even though they are just different manifestations of the same core issues.

Like many anorexics, I developed little checks to reassure myself I was okay, i.e. thin enough for the day. My basic check was to wrap my hand around my upper arm to make sure my middle finger would touch my thumb. At one point, my check was to feel my hip bones, something I did continually throughout the day, even though I knew it was impossible to gain enough weight to change that drastically in a few hours. These were rituals that, over time, became habit. There were also lies and rationalizations that constantly fell from my lips. They weren't outright intentional lies; "I ate earlier" didn't seem like lying. I just didn't tell anyone how much earlier it was when I last ate, and a "huge lunch" is all relative. My dedication to being honest was unintentionally waning and the line between reality and fantasy became more blurred in my head.

Looking back, I can see how I fooled myself in order to hang on to my eating disorder. I wanted to justify what I was doing, so that I didn't come off as sick to others. I rationalized and tried to explain away my quirky behaviors, hoping those around me wouldn't think I was anorexic. I don't think I was very convincing, but I continued trying to hide my disorder. Being on the other side of the illness, I now understand how frustrating it is to hear someone try to explain her strange behavior that doesn't support health with bizarre and irrational excuses.

When I see anorexic people today, I can detect rather quickly how far into the disease they are without taking great notice of their actual body weight. It's one of those "anorexics can't fool other anorexics" phenomena that occur once anorexia has been experienced on any level. It's obvious when the anorexic is visibly thin, but there are other indicators. Aside from the little checks they do, I can see the illness in the eyes. Anorexics have a certain look. If it's severe, the look is vacant. If the person is recovering, the look is pained and deep.

By the time I had my first seizure, I was completely lost. I had recently given most of my possessions away, thinking the end was near. I could feel myself slipping further and further away from the world around me. Consumed by obsessive-compulsive behavior, it was a struggle to make it through the day. It seemed that the thinner I got, the worse the OCD symptoms became. It got so that picking out an apple at the grocery store was an impossible task. I felt like Persephone seeking out prettier and prettier flowers in the fields. Each time I would settle on an apple I thought might be okay, I'd think maybe there was a better one. Only very rarely could I actually choose one that was acceptable. Finding the right one actually had little to do with size, shape or ripeness, it just had to "feel" right.

I'm sad to say that even after my first seizure, I wasn't ready to make an effort to get well. It would have been difficult even if I had been ready, because my finances were pretty well exhausted. Any treatment facility was out of the question. Besides, I felt I was losing the fight. Being healthy takes balls. Claiming the right to life and having radical trust in the universe is not for the weak. Embracing self-worth and self-wisdom takes an enormous amount of sheer strength and faith. I don't mean that in the typical religious sense, but faith nonetheless. Simply put, being human takes energy.

Because I had become so sick, I no longer felt like a woman. Even in high school, when I was so thin, I had a sense of my femininity. However, once I become so terribly emaciated, I felt asexual and made little effort to dress or care for myself except for basic hygiene. It was more important to me to remain thin than to evolve as a person, even though on some level I wanted to be well. The worst part during all of this was that I could feel my mind losing ground. Up until that point in my life, my mind had always been razor-sharp and overactive. Thoughts flooded my brain and creativity oozed from my very being. All of a sudden, I was living in a haze and experiencing things in slow motion. Then, horror of all horrors, I felt my thoughts escape the bounds of my own control.

As hard as I tried to focus my mind by reading or concentrating, I just couldn't. What I didn't know is that my serum sodium level was dangerously low; I had diluted my electrolytes through excessive water intake, and this condition – called hyponatremia – was causing my brain to short-circuit. Complete and utter panic grabbed me to my very soul and I knew something terrible was happening. Instead of calmness and nice white lights near-death survivors often claim to experience, I came face to face with paralysis, blackness and complete loss of control. After the seizures would pass, I would remember bits and pieces of the events leading up to the seizure itself; the tingle in my back, the repetitive thought that was stuck on replay, and the screaming that came from my mouth but seemed so far away.

Each visit to the hospital was expensive. The ambulance ride alone was close to $1,000 per trip. My insurance company had dropped me after my second hospital stay, so my parents footed the bill. After I was told the seizures were not exactly life-threatening, I wore a small necklace with a sign attached to it that read, "in case of seizure, please do not call an ambulance." After two trips, my parents couldn't afford to pay for another ride for me.

When I woke up one night to severe chest pain and shortness of breath, I thought for sure that was it. My mom and I took a cab to the hospital, where the doctors told her not to expect me to make it through the night. I begged them to find room for me at an eating-disorders treatment facility. Their response was, "Sorry, they're full." I looked at my mom and asked, "How sick do I have to be?" Clearly I was going to have to figure this out on my own. The real question was: Did I even want to get well?

* * *

PART III – White

Chapter 27 – Britta Kallevang

A poem by Britta Kallevang

I've never met a woman who could appear to be so grounded and confident, yet struggle with the very things that sent me over the edge. Because Britta was a runner, she was all too familiar with compulsive training and both food and body-image issues. Sometimes going through similar experiences can bond people together. I found a friend in Britta, and we both know that even when long expanses of time pass where we are not able to be in touch, we will always be there for one another. Britta has expressed some thoughts on her struggles in a completely different way: through poetry.

poems
&
poems
limbs
&
gut –
the head spins

        the rest
        is poles
        thick and thin
        and
        girth
        a horizontal
        plane
        fluxing
        up and down
        size

                tests its
                capabilities
                at taking
                over
                everyone
                and
                everything

and refers to
weight
it out
spin spin
so-called
what
is
this?

* * *

Chapter 28 – The Long Road

"Courage consists of the power of
self-recovery." – Julie Arabi

Anyone who has suffered an eating disorder can
tell you how increasingly distorted life becomes the
longer the illness progresses. It's hard to imagine being
so lost and so stuck that hope disappears. There was
a point in my illness where I had crossed over to what
I truly believed was a point of no return.

When I was younger, I was at least somewhat
well-rounded. I painted and drew, cooked, read
books and watched movies. I don't recall doing much

of anything once my weight became so abnormally low. I also don't recall exactly when it was that I stopped being in the world. I was isolated, except for a few select friends who could tolerate the sight of me, and I had dropped all hobbies and interests from my life. Days on end were spent exercising, though it's hard to imagine exercising with no real strength. I also spent my time waiting for my two small meals: one in the evening, one late at night. Occasionally, there were days I would eat more normally and even some days on which I would binge, but the guilt was extreme and often very hard to handle. At the time I couldn't see that those days of eating normally were what my body, mind and spirit craved.

Winters had always been hard on me, but when I weighed so little they became downright dreadful. I shivered in the top-of-the-line winter gear my mom had bought, freezing while others around me enjoyed the brisk air. Rather than risk another winter of extreme cold, I decided to seek warmer climates. Just a few months after being released from the hospital, I found a job at a Montessori school in Phoenix and left Boulder, hoping the new environment would not only ease the trauma of surviving harsh winters, but also allow me to escape my past. Yes, I was running away from my problems or at least attempting to escape. I wanted to get well, pay my parents back for all the money they spent on me and participate in the world again, but I couldn't face the possible comments from other people about any weight gain. My thinness was what defined me, and I knew from past experience how hard it would be to change. Understandably, well-meaning people who would say, "You look healthy" or "you've gained weight" did not know that for me, those words translated to "you're fat." Those were the words I knew would devastate me. I was hoping that if nobody knew me as an anorexic, I might be able to change. Instead, the new environment and added stress of living on my own caused me to revert back to my most compulsive regime in terms of both exercise and eating.

Instead of getting better, I got worse. My weight was just below 80 pounds at times, and I was constantly sick. Though the seizures had stopped, my immune system could not fight off colds, the flu, or any illness floating in the warm desert air. I missed many days of work at a time. During times of illness, my fevers would spike so high I worried for my life. I would shiver and sweat the nights away and wait for morning to come, hoping I would wake to see one more day yet tired of facing these days.

When I wasn't sick and merely trying to survive, I was compulsive, dragging myself through the days. I often called my sister or my friend, Heidi, in tears. I had no idea how selfish I was being at the time; all I could see was my own pain. I was miserable, living a marginal life. It took years before I could see the strain I put on others and how very much my friends and family suffered with my disorder. I had no idea of the sadness and anger my sister felt over losing her little sister who was, in fact, alive but not living. She felt cheated, not having a relative she could do things with, and admitted that she was tired of having to walk on eggshells around me, afraid that anything she said could upset me and potentially worsen or trigger my bad eating habits. She missed having someone she could do things with and talk to about things other than food and body image. It had been years since I had gone clothes shopping or gone out to eat with anyone. These were things my sister did with friends, because I wasn't able to be a part of her life with my distorted thinking.

People at work were concerned about me and often tried to encourage me to eat. I refused. I was good with the kids and I loved what I was doing, but at times I felt terribly weak. I was unable to lift or carry most of the children, and I remember disappointing one heavier boy when I couldn't lift him up onto the playground jungle gym. My heart went out to him, knowing exactly how he must have felt, but I was in no condition to be lifting the youngsters.

The kids where I worked were exceptional. They seemed wise beyond their years and had no problem making me feel welcome and wanted. To them it didn't matter what my weight was; they just wanted someone to listen to them, play with them and teach them. While basically getting paid to play with these kids, it occurred to me that I had really missed out as a child. Although I had played with the other kids in the neighborhood, I always felt like an outcast, not accepted. It was the first time other children wanted me to be a part of the group, even though I was an adult. I longed to have their innate wisdom regarding wants and needs and their sense of joy about life. Mostly, I longed to have their carefree attitude toward food.

One day, not long after settling into a regular routine of workouts and work, I noticed that one of my teeth was hurting. I made an appointment with a local dentist and he discovered a sinus infection. He also discovered that I had an infection on both sides of my upper jaw. Apparently, after all four of my wisdom teeth were removed many years earlier, an infection eventually developed in two of the empty tooth sockets. The dentist had to go back into the socket to clean out the infection. I was scheduled for surgery just a few days later. The surgery was long and draining. I was supposed to return to work the following week, but my face was so bruised and swollen on my already too-tiny body that the director of the school where I worked was afraid I would scare the children. I sat home for a few more days until the swelling subsided and returned only to have the kids comment on my terribly pale, slightly yellow complexion. It was becoming all too obvious that my anorexia was affecting my liver and I was jaundiced.

Not long after the surgery, I developed another injury. My diet continued to be incredibly unbalanced and I was still compulsively exercising, running on a sore leg and doing calisthenics. Eventually the pain got to be too much, so rather than fight it, I stopped running. In order to reduce the fear of gaining weight, I decided to try a few days of a modified juice fast. My daily intake consisted of vegetable juice plus a little brown rice and vegetables. No other solid foods were allowed. After a few days I was starving. I binged and purged and called in sick to work. I was a complete mess emotionally and physically. When I went into the bathroom to wash away the tears, I stared darkly at myself in the mirror, my self-hatred growing. My eyes penetrated the image in the mirror, looking deeply and critically at my reflection.

That's when it happened.

I had an epiphany. For the first time ever, and the last time since, I saw myself exactly as I was. I saw the bones on my face, my ribs sticking out, my thinning hair, my sharp hip bones protruding and my bony knees sticking out over my tiny calves. I could even see the bones between my almost nonexistent breasts where my ribs met. My arms were frail and so, so small. I was shocked, horrified. I was amazed I was still alive and finally understood all the stares and odd looks I received. I had no idea how things had gotten this bad, and I certainly had no idea how things could possibly get better. I knew I was stuck. I also knew I needed help.

* * *

"God comes to the hungry in the form of food." – *Mahatma Gandhi Quotes*, Mahatma Gandhi

As with any other addiction, anorexia is a means for someone whose life may feel out of control to establish a false sense of security. Unable to control events outside themselves, addicts control their immediate environment. There is considerable irony in that the addiction ultimately ends up controlling the individual, but there is comfort in knowing that the situation, as bad as it may become, won't change. Sometimes pain when one expects it is easier to handle than when outcomes are left up to fate. An extreme example of this is when victims of physically or verbally abusive perpetrators start an argument. Knowing when the slap or verbal attack is coming allows them to prepare for the blow and move on more quickly after the fact. Most often, a sense of the world being unpredictable stems from continually being let down by the universe; a parent failing to show love, a relationship ending abruptly, a lost job, a friend's death. Although addiction temporarily offers a sense of control, everyone knows life is something that can't really be driven and directed like some Hollywood movie. Going with the natural ebb and flow of nature is the best scenario, but is often a difficult exercise.

After a full day of crying and making calls to various counselors in the Phoenix area, I was told I could not receive financial assistance for any emotional or physical support or treatment until I was a resident. That meant I would have to stay there eight more months before I could afford care. I called my sister. I did not expect her to be so honest and forthright about how she felt. For the first time, she let me know that while she loved me and supported me, she was convinced that getting over an eating disorder was going to have to come from within. She was right; after all, I had spent thousands of dollars on hospitals, alternative medicine, books and therapists with no tangible results. I was like a chronic drunk who attends many Alcoholics Anonymous meetings without actually working the steps, assuming that something outside her could be the cure. While many of these avenues had given me greater insight into the disorder, none helped me overcome the problem. I understood my illness on an intellectual level, but I couldn't put it together in a way that allowed me to heal from it. I needed to take a leap of faith and allow myself to trust myself and trust that letting go didn't have to be such a struggle. There was a part of me that knew a healthier way to live, even if I couldn't visualize it perfectly. I had just never nurtured that part of me, because I was too caught up in punishing myself. I believed fully in Geneen Roth's method of living – listening to your body's inner wisdom and trusting that deep down, you know what your body needs. I knew in my heart everyone could learn to feel what hunger was and know when fullness occurred. What I didn't realize at the time, though, was the physiology behind eating and fullness and how much that changes with prolonged food issues.

In normal people, when blood sugar drops, the liver sends signals to the hypothalamus alerting the brain that the body needs glucose, the sugar the body breaks down from food. At this point, physical hunger is often experienced when the stomach contracts and the urge to find food and eat is experienced. The hypothalamus also identifies particular foods your body needs and is thought to be responsible for cravings. After food has been consumed, hormones are released and again find their way to the hypothalamus as the food begins to move from the stomach into the intestines. These hormones tell the body it's time to stop eating. One hormone, called leptin, is released from the fat cells themselves. Satiety occurs after all these hormones have traveled to the hypothalamus. Unfortunately, with both starvation and purging, it's as if these hormones become downright confused and are hesitant to be released. It takes a much longer time for leptin to be released in a bulimic than in a normal person. This can often trigger another binge because the bulimic actually still feels hungry, despite having just eaten a normal meal. Since anorexics constantly override these hunger signals, hormonal chaos results and delayed hormone release is likely. It takes many weeks of regular meals to establish the hormonal connection that allows one to begin to read and recognize both hunger and fullness. It has been reported that some of the concentration-camp victims in World War II experienced a warped sense of body image. It is also known that some who survived starvation and the harsh conditions of the camps ate so much upon their release their stomachs burst. Clearly, the body this far out of balance is not able to regulate its own needs for survival.

After much consideration, I decided to move back to Boulder where I could at least find support from family and friends. In the meantime, I was determined to allow my body to rule my appetite. I figured I had already hit rock bottom, so anything, even gaining weight, could not be as bad as living the way I had been living. To celebrate my faith that I would survive and live to see a better life, I went out for ice cream, something I had not done in over 10 years. I had sometimes eaten frozen yogurt at home, but to actually go out and allow someone else to serve me was something I had not experienced since my days in college.

I remembered from my stay in the hospital that once my metabolism started working again, I would be hungry. I didn't realize I would experience an almost frantic need for food. I would eventually have to address both the emotional deprivation and the extreme physical deprivation the years and years of anorexia had caused. At times I would become panicky at the thought of having to wait to eat. I was consuming food every few hours. When I packed my belongings and headed home, I was on a mission to eat exactly what I craved. On my drive to Colorado, I stopped at five different stores in search of a bran muffin. It took an extra hour to find one, but after such severe restriction, I was allowing myself some indulgences. My fear of gaining weight was definitely still right in my face, but it was as if my body had taken over. I didn't fight my intense cravings, only the thoughts in my head that insisted I was already getting fat.

Unfortunately, after too many sugary meals and far too little protein, I set myself up for another short bout of bulimia. It seemed that no matter how much I ate, it wasn't enough. Also, for some reason, I couldn't exercise without crying. It was as if all my fears were coming back to haunt me. I buckled under the past trauma of performing and overtraining, starving and living compulsively. My self-esteem was shot to hell and I was desperate for reassurance that I was going to be okay. I followed my mom around like a little puppy dog in order to feel safe. I felt vulnerable and shy and was having a terrible time trying to regulate my food intake. It seemed that the pendulum had swung in the complete opposite direction and stayed there after being held so tightly on one side. I finally saw a psychiatrist who put me on an antipsychotic drug called clozapine and some antidepressants, including a low dose of Prozac.

Eventually I started to reach some balance. I felt obese at just around 95 pounds, only 15 pounds heavier than my low point. This was still very thin, but my weight was creeping ever higher and my fear was that it wouldn't stop increasing. My psychiatrist told me that one of two things would happen: Either I'd continue to be anorexic or I'd get healthy and end up hating my body. This was a Sophie's choice, and I didn't believe him. I also couldn't believe he would say something like that. I knew there were women out there who were healthy and tolerated their bodies. I had even heard of people who actually loved their bodies. I refused to accept those as my only two choices. I quit seeing him and attempted to take responsibility for my own wellness.

Since I was still struggling with a horrible self-image, despite my belief that others could overcome this issue, I decided that in addition to starting to run again, I was going to stop weighing myself. I could not deal with the numbers any longer. They made me crazy no matter what objective story they told, and I obsessed about being a certain weight when the scale was involved. It's terrible to consider how a number could determine how I felt about myself. I knew this then, yet I still couldn't stand the thought of my weight going above that 100-pound mark. I tried hard to stick to some sort of regular eating pattern: breakfast, lunch, dinner, and one snack. It wasn't long before I couldn't stand the sight of myself, though, and I started restricting again.

The next few months were a roller coaster of eating what I felt was too much and then reverting back to sharply restricting calories. I was running again and back to working out several hours a day, mixing the running with biking, walking and calisthenics. It wasn't long before I was struck down with another stress fracture in my pubic bone. A later diagnosis would show that, over the years, I had suffered several small fractures in addition to the larger one in that area. I took to biking and lifting. I was very shocked at how weak I was. I had no core strength despite all the running and compulsive aerobic exercise, which only burned what little muscle tissue I'd retained. My muscles did not seem to respond to weight training by getting bigger or stronger. Instead, they broke down. It was as if my body no longer knew how to synthesize muscle. I experienced chronic soreness in addition to a general feeling of not moving forward and feeling stuck, yet I continued to work out like a hamster trapped on a wheel.

A therapist friend of mine and I decided that since I had a tendency toward bipolar disorder, I should stop the antidepressants. She suggested lithium, but I was too afraid of the possible weight gain. I already felt such self-loathing at just over 100 pounds. I couldn't imagine gaining more weight and living with myself. I had stopped purging, but was still having difficulty finding balance. On a whim, I tried a product called SAM-e. I didn't notice any great change at first, so I stopped taking it, but a month or so later I realized it had actually been easing the depression I had felt throughout my life.

As for my eating, a combination of what I thought was sensible and what my body was craving seemed the best approach, so I used a variation of the Zone Diet to achieve at least some sort of regularity in my life. I found that eating smaller meals throughout the day kept me from feeling panicky or overly worried. The smaller, more frequent meals kept me from getting overly hungry or weak and also helped keep metabolism going. The smaller meals were also much easier to digest and didn't leave me feeling as bloated or full. To help keep my blood-sugar levels from fluctuating too much, I made sure not to eliminate entire food groups from my diet. Basically, instead of following any diet in particular, I learned to balance what I was craving with a sensible meal plan. I aimed for a bit of protein, carbohydrate and fat at each meal. Still, I relied heavily on calorie-counting strictly out of fear of gaining too much weight, and letting go completely seemed out of the question.

A few months later, when my stress fracture had healed, I began running again, and I decided I wanted to run a marathon. I knew it was risky, but I wanted to prove to myself that I had the ability to give my body what it needed to run that far. I wanted to prove to myself I could adapt. I needed to show the people around me I had courage, so I started training by running longer runs on the weekends. I knew that on some level I was a bit over the edge but considering where I had been, I was indeed healthier, at least emotionally.

During the time I trained for the marathon I met some amazing new people, people who showed me the meaning of true friends. Unaware I was continually complaining about how fat I felt, I was confronted by my running partners. They said that while they loved me, they didn't want to hear me say "I feel fat" anymore. This led to a change in my conversational habits that ultimately helped ease the actual feeling. The more I moved away from saying that I felt fat, the more I moved away from actually feeling fat. Eventually, I even thought about it less. The noise of these obsessive thoughts was decreasing over time. When I began to have panic attacks, another friend, Misty, suggested I wasn't eating enough. She pointed out the pattern of my panic attacks and suggested I try eating a bit more each day. She said, "Look, you know that what you're doing isn't working, so just change." I laughed, "What?" I couldn't "just change." Or could I? I had never thought about it, but she was right. "Just try something different for a week, and if it doesn't work, you can always go back to what you were doing before," Misty said. "Chances are, though, you won't want to. If all else fails, try something completely different" And all of a sudden, I saw not one way out, but many. Infinite options were before me.

Change is hard for most people. It's even more of a challenge for anorexics. They tend to set rules in concrete and develop rituals that may appear meaningless to others but are as essential as a life-sustaining breath of air to them. In addition, they are some of the best game-players in the world. No matter the extent to which rules around food, deprivation, and exercise threaten their lives, they will do what it takes to stay the course. It's easy for an outsider to suggest that they just eat something, simply change the rules, but this is nearly impossible for someone trapped in the grip of such an illness. The desire to be well may be there, but the means to becoming well is missing. The thought of simply eating something outside the rules set is just not an option. There is no going cold turkey with anorexia. Unlike stopping other addictions, it's impossible to have an all-or-nothing avenue for recovery. Instead, it's more a matter of gradual change, baby steps. Although the analogy of a smoker having to smoke only half a cigarette is not quite accurate because cigarettes are not ultimately healthy for the body, in terms of addiction, the difficulty of this scenario would compare to what an anorexic has to do in order to recover.

When it comes to eating disorders, it often takes someone outside to allow for the permission of a change in the rule book. At times when exhaustion from dealing with the disorder and all that it brings sets in, an anorexic will welcome outside help and agree that someone other than herself needs to step in and take control. It takes an enormous amount of strength for this change to come from within. Whether the initial change happens as the result of allowing someone else to take control or from allowing the body's needs to finally be heard, it is the only thing that will ultimately lead to recovery. Finding self-worth and discovering self-love are integral parts of reclaiming health. Simply gaining weight is not the cure to anorexia, and it's essential to feel worthy in order to heal. Listening to the inner self – the self that longs to live and be free and play by rules that are not so strict – is the real cure.

Anorexics have a tendency to see the world in black and white. It's either-or; there's no living in the grey. It occurred to me in the middle of my conversation with Misty that eating didn't have to be a matter of starving or being fat; it could possibly be something in between. With this broad new view of my once-limited world, I was able to occasionally add snacks to my daily diet as needed. The panic attacks were fairly manageable and seemed to lessen with proper nutrition and by avoiding caffeine. The panic attacks would eventually get worse, but at the time they were not overly worrisome. I finished the marathon almost completely anonymously in an unimpressive time of 3:49 that included two stops – one to talk to a friend on the sidelines and one to use the portable toilet – but I found that I had accomplished a great feat. I had discovered my ability to listen to my body.

I would find out later that listening to my body could be disrupted and would become nearly impossible with so much damage already done to it. For some unknown reason, my body was continuing to break down despite an improved diet and a strict "no purging" policy; it was as if I had passed some physical point of no return, like a former smoker who quits too late to keep her emphysema from gradually worsening in spite of having given up cigarettes. And so it was that just when I thought I was getting on my feet, I faced the fact that despite not yet being 35 years old, I might have already caused irreversible damage to my body.

* * *

Chapter 30 – Living to Die

"[W]e now know that the human animal is characterized by two great fears that other animals are protected from: the fear of life and the fear of death... Heidegger brought these fears to the center of his existential philosophy. He argued that the basic anxiety of [humanity] is anxiety about being-in-the-world, as well as anxiety of being-in-the-world. That is, both fear of death and fear of life, of experience and individuation." – Ernest Becker

It seems a bizarre irony that someone so afraid of death would have taken her life right up to the edge for a possible glimpse of the other side. Perhaps I thought I was facing my fear. Regardless, confronting the reality that I might soon die – which I had to do more than once – never actually eased my intense phobia. If anything, it only made it worse. When I was in the throes of anorexia, I would often consider that any given moment could be my last. However, I was never able to let go of all the limitations and restrictions I had placed on myself. I had a bad case of the what-might-bes. I would think of all the foods I had missed tasting, all the life I had missed living, and all the people I had missed meeting. My life had become so narrow, uneventful and gloomy. I needed to know how the story would end, and I didn't want it to end like it was threatening to. It took years for me to reach any kind of balance and start sampling life again. Just as I was beginning to emerge from the ugly black pit of my past, I was struck with the intense feeling I was going to die.

There have been several times in my life when I have come face-to-face with death. The first incident was in grade school. I was at home playing with a friend and suddenly felt a terrible headache coming on. The headache was so bad that I had to ask my friend to leave so I could go lie down. The pain intensified quickly. Before I could even attempt to call out to my mom down the hallway in the other room, I became paralyzed from the severe throbbing pressure growing in my skull. It was as if my brain was going to explode. Any slight movement was far too painful to tolerate, so I stayed as still as possible for over an hour until my mom finally came looking for me. When she entered the room, I saw her panicked face as she leaned over me. My eyes had glazed over and we both thought I would be dead shortly. "My head," I managed to whisper. She called the hospital, but the nurse told her there was an epidemic of viral meningitis going around. Chances were I was another case. The hospital was swamped. My mom was told to call back only if I didn't improve over the next three hours and an ambulance would be sent. Viral meningitis is described as a swelling of the outer layer of the brain. It is extremely painful and can cause brain damage, deafness, blindness, and in some instances, death. Fortunately, the pain lessened over the course of the night, and it was indeed, as the ER operator had expected, viral meningitis and not a related – but often lethal – disease, bacterial meningitis. I recovered fully over the next few days and was back to my normal activity in less than a week. Many years later, when I was in my early forties, I would be struck down again with this illness in a much more severe case. Miraculously, in the latter case, after nine days in the hospital with my life hanging in the balance, I was released and started a slow recovery. As a friend of the family put it, "You have bad luck." However, I have to recognize that living in a state of malnutrition for so long probably didn't help me have good luck when it comes to health.

Another brush with death I experienced was in college, when I went river-rafting with a few friends. It was my first experience in a raft. I had grand images of sunning myself on a spacious raft on the calm waters. When the river guide started pumping up the tiny inflatable vessels by hand, my daydream came to a disappointing halt.

I should have figured out that the trip was cursed when, as we were waiting to shove off into the mild waters, a big spider crawled over my hand. We split up into two teams, and just as my team was beginning to get the hang of maneuvering the tiny little raft, the guide yelled out for us to paddle as hard as we could. I heard a loud roar of rushing water before us, and as I lifted my oar out of the water fully intending to plunge it back in as hard as I possibly could, the raft flipped and I was sucked under. My first instinct was to fight to reach the surface, but I was being pulled under with such force, I knew that any effort would be futile. A strange calm took over me as I looked up and saw the raft getting farther and farther away. I convinced myself that the force pulling me down had to stop at some point. I was right. The moment I felt the eddy release me, I swam for the surface with a fury that I had never known before. I could see the sun on the water above me. It seemed so incredibly far away though. I was completely out of breath with a good three feet left to swim. Time stood still and all was quiet just before I broke into the air and sputtered and coughed as the guide quickly maneuvered the raft to me and pulled me aboard.

As traumatic as this was, it was my most serene confrontation with death to date. Somehow the thought of nature being in control had, at that moment, eased my worries about death. The force of nature was something I realized then that I couldn't fight. If the eddy had continued to pull me under, it was beyond my control to fight. This sense of serenity in the hands of some universal force did not, however, transfer to the relatively microscopic environment of my own body. Once I became anorexic, the seizures and near-death experiences were filled with terror and fear, and just when I thought it was all behind me, I once again came face-to-face with my own mortality.

After I ran my first marathon, I started to experience severe stiffness in my pelvis, hamstrings, lower back and hips. It was such an accomplishment to have finished the marathon, regardless of my time. Despite running much more slowly than I had in the past, I felt satisfied and even a little bit emotional crossing the finish line. Unfortunately, shortly after the race, everything started to hurt, and I could hardly step up a single stair riser normally, let alone jog. It didn't make sense that I would be this sore when I hadn't truly raced the marathon and even stopped twice. I saw over 11 practitioners, from chiropractors to medical doctors, none of whom could offer any help or provide a clue as to what was going on in my body. In addition to the chronic stiffness, I was beginning to experience panic attacks. I was worried the seizures were coming back, but I couldn't figure out why they would occur since my weight and electrolytes were stable. The attacks started fairly mildly; I would get a funny sensation in my back and experience a sense of worry and fear. I tried in vain to reassure myself everything was okay, that I was going to be fine, but the attacks got progressively worse. Eventually I was getting full-blown fight-or-flight responses for no apparent reason.

At this time I was working as a nanny for two fun, outgoing kids in addition to working part-time at a local health-food store. I had to miss a few days of work when the panic became severe, and I noticed both chest pain and shortness of breath. Convinced I had wrecked my body and was paying for my anorexic past, I assumed I was about to have a heart attack. I went to the emergency room in tears with the distinct feeling I was going to die. I was very scared. The fear seemed beyond my control; no amount of positive self-talk could ease my worries and physical symptoms.

For so many years, I had been living in limbo. It seemed unfair that death would squeeze its icy fingers around my heart just at the time I was deciding I wanted to live and not merely exist. In the past, I had lived by default: too afraid to actually kill myself, but equally afraid to really be in the world. I had fallen to a certain level of mediocrity, no longer a heroic athlete or super student. I felt I had failed Life 101. I was thin though, and that meant something. It seemed it was the only thing over which I had any control. Here I was, finally stepping up to experience all I had been missing, and there was death staring at me once again. For the first time in over five years, I was starting to feel again. I even had a slight crush on one of the guys at the health-food store and had gone on my first date in what felt like an eternity. I remember our first kiss like it was my first ever. Suddenly a door that had been closed was thrown open, and I was aware of my own sexuality. The thought of a heart attack sickened me and made me realize my own fate was out of my hands. Eating more or eating less would not solve this problem. I realized how little control one actually does have in life.

The doctor who saw me that day reassured me that my heart was beating fine. She did detect a clicking sound and ordered an ultrasound, which revealed a heart-valve leak. She called it mitral valve prolapse and told me the condition itself actually causes panic attacks. What occurs is a physical response, not a mental or emotional episode. I was instructed to give up chocolate, caffeine, teas and any stimulants and watch my blood-sugar levels. Homeostasis was best for keeping the panic attacks and other symptoms at bay.

With the panic attacks resolved, I was left to once again deal with the pain and stiffness issue. I had started running again in order to train for another marathon or perhaps a half-marathon, but I suffered on my long runs. I shuffled and limped along with my running partners and had trouble keeping up. Running with my new circle of friends had previously allowed me to open up and feel more at ease with myself. However, the pain was forcing me to shut down a bit. Once the chatterbox of the group, I had become quiet and would often fall so far back that my training buddies had to circle around to pick me up again. After a failed attempt to run a half-marathon, I decided to get a coach and see another chiropractor. These would be two of the best moves I ever made in my life.

* * *

Chapter 31 – Bobby

"Coaching is a profession of love. You can't coach people unless you love them." – Eddie Robinson

I met Bobby shortly after I had run my marathon. He agreed to be my coach despite the fact that I was still struggling with food and body issues. In addition, I was injured and could hardly walk at the time. Bobby was convinced that the two of us could create a healthier path to running again for me, and his passion

and optimism rubbed off on me so much that I even
thought for a brief moment I was ready to let go
completely of the illness that I had clung to for the
majority of my life. Though this freedom never quite
occurred, Bobby did help me begin to express myself
more and ultimately opened a door to a much happier
life. His constant and unconditional support allowed
me to begin to investigate my own self-worth,
something that had been completely and totally torn
apart by past traumas and the internalization of harsh
comments by others. Though we no longer work
together as coach and athlete, we remain closely
bonded as friends. I'll let him tell our story:

> Firstly let me say that it is both an
> honor and a privilege to have worked
> with Lize as her running coach and now to
> be her friend. This leads into what I feel is
> the most effective asset in the process of
> being a support to those unfortunate
> enough to suffer the horrors of anorexia –
> empathy. Remember, I am only a running
> coach with training in sport psychology,
> hardly the credentials I needed when it
> came about that I became someone
> known for having some insight and facility
> with anorexic distance runners.
> I was fortunate enough to realize
> very early on in my work with these
> athletes that the running was often likely to

be the compulsion that had replaced that abhorrence for food.

From a plain exercise physiological point of view, the lighter the runner the higher their Vo2Max. This is their ability (measured in milliliters) to utilize oxygen per kilogram of body weight. This is a key performance factor in endurance events. The lighter the athlete therefore, the better they perform – hence the warped "reward" that these athletes receive for losing so much weight. Of course this period of heightened performance is finite as the effects of the illness start to shut down the system with its all-too-often inevitable outcome – terrible, terrible illness, anguish and even death.

At the risk of sounding simplistic, let me lay out the loose process I follow when an athlete entrusted me with the truth of their condition:

Never view the illness as a simple case of misaligned thinking that can easily be corrected by a nice logical heart-to-heart conversation.

Gain permission from the athlete to be forthright – negotiate the space to be honest. When working with athletes who have clearly dealt with the illness since their youth, I often request to speak with the "adult," when it is clear that the "child" is very much present in a trying/challenging situation.

Be wary of creating false hope as to the length of time or the possible linear course that the healing process may take.

Have a healthy take on the curability of the disease – I told myself that an athlete is either in remission (and working damn hard at it), or caught in the throes of the thing. Thinking that a runner (or any anorexic person for that matter), is fully and finally cured is a fallacy that can lull the supporters of the person into dropping their guard and miss crucial clues that could help prevent another acute phase.

Be utterly constant and unconditional in your love and support. Also be unwavering in the standards you set as acceptable; for example I refuse to offer coaching when the athlete is below a medically determined minimum weight. I never, however, dropped the athlete from my program when this occurred, only refused to allow them to train.

I would only coach such athletes with the existence of a team consisting of the coach, psychologist (or some effective type of psychotherapist) and a nutritionist. I would not move forward without the okay from these two persons. Of course, all these team members had to be totally trusted and accepted by the athlete. The athlete also has to be totally okay with open and clear communication between the three support members, other than the usual accepted confidences that these specialists must abide by.

Lastly, let me say that I coach by agreement and never more so than with the condition of anorexia. If an athlete trusts me, I honor that trust for the duration of the coaching relationship and beyond.

I hope that these thoughts are of some use to others who are part of the world of anorexia.

For many, there is a set belief that an anorexic can never fully overcome the illness. A coach must constantly keep an eye on anyone who has struggled with eating issues in the past. It's very easy for someone who has had an eating disorder to start sliding back into bad eating patterns when training or stepping back into competition. Most people who have had struggles with food and weight do better with a positive, one-on-one coaching style that avoids punishment or negative feedback based on performance. The focus with these kinds of athletes should clearly be more on motivation and personal achievements than on weight. Training and racing at the elite level can put an athlete at risk for developing an eating disorder. With good coaching and guidance, an athlete can remain healthy while reaching their athletic goals.

* * *

Chapter 32 – The End Result

"The day the child realizes that all adults are imperfect, he becomes an adolescent; the day he forgives them, he becomes an adult; the day he forgives himself, he becomes wise" – Alden Nowlan

The long-term effects of eating disorders are not pretty. Because of prolonged malnourishment, anorexics and bulimics are at risk for an inexhaustible list of related complications. I was fortunate in a way to have avoided becoming fully immersed in bulimia. During a few transitional phases of my life, I did binge and purge, but I was able to completely stop and I have not thrown up since 1998. Bulimia is a vicious illness that can cause esophageal damage, irritation or bleeding in the stomach lining, and erosion of the enamel on the teeth. I have known girls who have ruptured blood vessels in their eyes, passed out and developed ulcers. Other risks include dehydration, electrolyte and mineral imbalance, edema, fluid on the lungs, cancer of the esophagus or throat, high blood pressure and diabetes. Ketoacidosis, a condition in which acids build up in blood as a result of the body burning fat instead of sugar and carbohydrates to get energy, is also probable. In addition, it can lead to pancreatitis. Bulimia comes with a financial cost as well. At times, the craving to binge can cause those suffering from the disorder to spend huge amounts on food. When money runs out, some even resort to stealing. And to top it off, some bulimics report worsening bouts of acne during binge-purge cycles.

It's a heartbreaking reality that anorexia is striking younger and younger victims today. It is not uncommon for children of eight or nine years old to be refusing food at dinner tables across the country. It's exceptionally disturbing to know that these young kids are denying their bodies important nutrients at a critical growing phase in their lives. Although talking about anorexia has become more acceptable these days, this has not helped solve the problem, and the incidence of young children with anorexia has increased at such an alarming rate that treatment centers have had to add special units specifically for kids under the age of 12. Starvation at any age is a recipe for disaster, but denying the body food at a time when the body is growing can lead to permanent and irreversible damage and is more likely to lead to death.

In a world where high-powered superkids like Mary-Kate Olsen set the standard for hot pre-teen fashion, it's all too easy for young children to follow the unhealthy Hollywood trend. However, society's influence and insistence that it's okay to be malnourished isn't the only thing that leads a child to refuse food. There are many factors that contribute to any illness or addiction. In the case of anorexia, it was once thought the disease was entirely an emotional response to events outside the individual or the result of poor parenting. Many psychiatrists thought anorexia typically occurred just before puberty and that victims were afraid to grow up. It's true that many people with addictions fear taking on adult responsibilities. The "Peter Pan syndrome" may play a small part in some cases of anorexia, but recently it has been discovered that there is a genetic predisposition which can lead to anorexia. Just like alcoholism, it's a very complex illness and can have many triggers that may lead an individual to self-destruct. It's true that many of the affected girls I knew had similar traits, such as being raped or abused in their pasts, but today similarities among sufferers of anorexia are becoming less apparent. Where once anorexia was thought to be a rich, white girl's disease, it is now crossing the gender gap as well as knocking aside ethnic and economic barriers.

Despite all of my chronic pain and stiffness, I continued to run and work out up to three hours a day. On some level I was hoping for a late comeback, on another, I was using training as an excuse to feel okay about myself. I was aware this compulsiveness was also keeping me centered in some way. I still had a hard time allowing myself to eat normally if I didn't work out. No matter how much I believed the body needs food at rest as well as when it's at work, I experienced a tremendous amount of guilt on rest days. I have heard others with anorexia say that the illness is a way to say to the world, "I'm not okay." Typically, anorexics display the traits of perfection. They are intelligent, hard working, successful, and loyal. Their frail outer appearance, however, is a reflection of their inner turmoil. They hold an underlying core belief they are ugly and worthless, not even deserving enough to take up space in the world. Although at this point in my life, I appeared to be recovering, I was continuing to bump up against these very issues. With the full intention of getting back into racing shape, I looked into hiring a local coach. I had several friends helping me with certain aspects of my training, but I was looking for someone who could deal with the emotional runner that I was; someone who could handle what had pushed most other people out of my life.

When I called Bobby, I knew immediately I had found the right coach. We met to discuss my goals and past training. I didn't hide anything and told him I was extremely fearful of running and my own traumatic past. I still had periods where I would cry on runs, feeling overwhelmed and helpless against the demons in my head. I was still struggling with counting calories and obsessive-compulsive habits, but Bobby offered me some hope. We agreed to work together on a running program. In addition, I was lucky enough to find a chiropractor who was able to help ease some the stiffness and pain I was experiencing enough so I could run more normally again.

Running with Bobby brought some of the joy back into my training. It was obvious that I was very traumatized, not only by my own starvation but also by the lack of unconditional love and support from many people in my past. It took someone who was not attached to how fast I ran to make me see that. Bobby gave me unconditional support no matter how I performed and, as a result, I started running a bit faster again. Long gone were the days of running 5k's at 5:30 pace, but 6:45 wasn't so bad given what I had been through. I understood this, but deep down I still deemed my slippage into mediocrity unacceptable. I was completely unsatisfied in my races and felt hindered and limited by my own body. Never before had I struggled on such a physical level with running. It felt as if I were a rusty car falling apart or a racehorse with a broken leg, limping to the finish line. I naturally had vivid memories of the runner I'd been in high school and couldn't accept where I now was in comparison. Never did I imagine I could let go of running, so I held on and struggled through workouts and even easy runs, my body filled with pain and my mind brimming with disappointment.

Where I was once a confident racer, bold and a real risk-taker, I had become limited and timid and very afraid. My stride had completely changed, as if to verify my fears of continually being let down. Gone were the fierce steps carrying a heartfelt "I'll show you" message. Instead, my feet were landing timidly, searching for the ground below as if it might just fall away, a definite "don't hurt me" statement. It was during another injury, oddly enough, where I found some of my lost fierceness. Rather than drop me as an athlete when I developed a stress fracture in my foot, Bobby supported me and offered to give me bike workouts in replacement. With no worries about my performance and nobody watching, I was able to push some limits and get my heart rate up to racing levels. At times I rode with reckless abandon and it felt good to find some of the fire inside me that had been missing for so long.

Unfortunately, the stress fracture took a long time to heal. After two weeks of doing my best to stay off it, I went to a podiatrist in Longmont, Colorado to see if a cast might help the bone heal. The podiatrist insisted that I didn't have a stress fracture. My coach, physical trainer and I all felt otherwise. I had even been to a bone specialist who said he felt sure it was a stress fracture as well. After a bit of arguing, the podiatrist took and x-ray which did not show any cracks in my bones. I knew from past experience that stress fractures don't usually show up on an x-ray until they have started to heal, sometimes up to three or four weeks later, but this guy was convinced that I had a neuroma. He felt there was inflammation in my foot, so he gave me a shot of cortisone and told me I could run in three days. Two days later, my foot made an odd popping noise, and I collapsed to the floor in excruciating pain. The podiatrist said he had no idea what was wrong. He suggested wrapping my foot in a soft cast or casting my entire leg from my knee to my toe in hard plaster. I knew there had to be another option, so after several days of limping around, my foot throbbing with intense pain, I went for a second opinion. "You have a stress fracture," the second podiatrist said, immediately putting me in a removable walking cast. An x-ray confirmed this. The fracture took another six weeks to heal, but my left foot would never be the same again. I've had two surgeries to clean up the osteoarthritis in my joints that were badly damaged after the cortisone caused my tendons to atrophy severely. To this day, my foot still rolls out and I have a slight limp.

In spite of the fact I was dealing with yet another injury, I noticed that something was different. It's hard to say what exactly changed in my life. Perhaps it was the unconditional acceptance from others that I was starting to feel or feeding myself the nutrients that by body craved. It happened gradually, but what I noticed was that despair no longer ruled my life. Before long I started to emerge as a new person. The changes were subtle at first, but I was laughing more and feeling more at ease in my body, calmer in my mind. I was even getting out and being social again. I often wondered if I was really the same little fat girl I was as a child, the standout runner I was in high school, or the scared woman who nearly died. Then it struck me that maybe I had left these all behind and become someone entirely new. For the first time in my life I felt like I could breathe a sigh of relief. I was beginning to show myself compassion and kindness instead of brutality and hatred. I realized that I was, in fact, the same person inside whether I was eighty pounds or one hundred and ten pounds, but I had grown and learned, expanded beyond my illness. In addition, I found that one hundred and ten pounds, give or take, allowed me to be more involved in the world. Somewhere inside me is the core of who I am. It doesn't change with outer appearance. Reclaiming this inner core has helped tremendously with recovery. It was important for me to rediscover likes, dislikes, passions and any opinions I had that I'd put aside to be an anorexic girl. As a child, I was unable to self-regulate under the tremendous stress of my home life. Anorexia was the addiction I chose to help me cope with my surroundings and anything beyond my control.

It wasn't until I was in my thirties that I began to rediscover my voice. I had just started to volunteer at a local radio station when I realized that I had something to say. I had an opinion about what music I like and disliked, and there were issues that interested me. While I had been quiet and shut-down for years, it seemed, I suddenly felt the urge to jump into debates and heated conversations. It amazed me that all of the years I spent focusing on weight and food had pushed me so far away from myself as well as others. It was time to reclaim myself, and that meant finding out who I am. I was ready to be heard, and I was finally ready to be alive. There was a feeling of safety being behind the mike without anyone looking at me. I was comfortable getting in touch with my wilder side, and it was fun. I didn't feel judged in any way.

Going through puberty is not easy. It's even more difficult as an adult. At age 33 I had gone nearly 20 years without a period. From the time I was 14, I didn't have a cycle. I did take hormones for a very brief time that were incredibly hard on my body and that induced one period when I was in college, but I quickly stopped when the PMS symptoms got to be too much. I experienced severe bloating, cramping and terrible headaches. In my early thirties when my first period did come, it was harsh. I could feel my body changing and noticed symptoms of PMS for months before the actual period came. I felt awkward and uncomfortable as my breast size increased and my body adjusted to the new level of hormones. With anorexia, hormone levels decrease, especially estrogen and testosterone. This was clearly a sign that my body, at least in one aspect, was becoming healthier. One day, I thought I had the flu. I was forced to stay in bed for two days. At that time I got my period. I thought it was a coincidence that I had the flu, but the next month there I was in bed again with the flu. It turned out that my body was having such a hard time adjusting to becoming a woman that I was thrown into fits of fevers and aches and other flu-like symptoms with every cycle. Over the course of a year, the periods started to become more regular and less traumatic.

Through all these changes and the growth I experienced, Bobby was supportive. When my foot healed and I was back to running, I entered a cycle of continual set-backs. Bobby didn't flinch; he stuck with me and offered an enormous amount of emotional support. It soon became apparent that my body was not reacting in a normal way to training. I was experiencing random muscle shutdown and chronic fatigue, and unrelenting stiffness lingered in my body. I was back on the trail of seeking out healers and therapists at a time when I felt all these issues should have resolved themselves. My body felt broken. I was tired, stressed and weak, and over the course of the next two years, it only got worse. The one thing that kept me going was hope. I was convinced there was a solution to my health problems, and I was determined to find it.

* * *

"In the midst of winter, I finally learned that there was in me an invincible summer." - – Albert Camus

I met Patty Murray when I was at the tail end of my college career. She was a well-known runner then, but she was also struggling with anorexia. I hadn't kept up with her career once my own struggles became so severe, but when I started to recover, I was fortunate enough to see her at the track one day, running well and looking strong. I was very anxious to meet her and hear how she recovered from anorexia, so we decided to meet for coffee and an interview. It is, after all, rare to find someone who has completely and totally recovered from this illness. However, from our brief conversation on the phone, it sounded like Patty was one of those incredible examples.

When Patty and I sat down on an exceptionally warm fall day, I immediately noticed that despite having the lean body of a true athlete, her eyes were sparkling and clear. In addition, based on our brief chat before the interview began, it was obvious that her mind was occupied not with thoughts of food, weight and exercise, but with spring cleaning and other plans for the day ahead. Already I was in awe. This was a woman who had at one point weighed around 80 pounds, and there seemed to be no trace of any kind of illness lingering within her.

As a standout runner in high school, Patty developed anorexia that eventually caused her running career to come to a halt. Her coach had suggested that she lose 10 to 15 pounds, and Patty had gone too far. Despite running well for a while, she eventually became too weak, and her family encouraged her to seek treatment. She stayed in a hospital where she was watched around the clock. At 5'2" and only 80 pounds, her doctors told her she should never run again and feared that a return to training would lead her to relapse into anorexia. To the shock and disbelief of those around her, Patty was eventually able to find her stride and get back on track with both her life and her running.

There was a time shortly after Patty was released from the hospital where she was forced to find a job and support herself. No longer able to entertain thoughts of maintaining a career as a professional runner, she quit training for several years, and concentrated on work and making ends meet. In addition, Patty started socializing and going out. "I completely changed my life to where I was going out with friends and going dancing," she says. She actually gained weight during this time and got up to about 110 pounds. When she decided to start running again, she knew she was in a better place to do so. "I took all those years off and realized that it wasn't really me. I wasn't into the partying and all that. I like to run, so I decided to start up again," Patty says. For Patty, it was a different atmosphere, and her focus was more on enjoying running, not competition.

When I asked Patty how she recovered and to identify some of the key factors that made this remarkable return to health possible, she said, "It's almost like I'm a whole different person. It's hard to explain. For a while I ate kind of funny, not normal like I do now. I don't even think about it any more at all, it seems as though I'm one of those one-in-a-million people who recover. I see pictures of myself from the past and I think I looked horrible. That helps me keep doing what I'm doing, because I feel better and think I look better, too. I also don't weigh myself; I go more on how I feel and how much energy I have. When I see others with anorexia, I think it's sad. I know that it doesn't have to be like that. In terms of running, I think women take a healthier approach today. Times have changed." It's true, I agreed. Now women are starting to focus on how they feel rather than how thin they are, but it's only just beginning. There are still those who falsely believe, "the thinner the better."

Despite her more relaxed attitude toward running, Patty eventually did start racing again. In fact, in 2008 she won the national masters 10k title by running 34:50. "I've been happy to just enjoy running," she states. What I noticed is that Patty is not merely a runner. Her life seems well-rounded and complete. She is able to go with the flow and has other things in her life to occupy her time and thoughts: a relationship, work, social time, and general living.

* * *

"Our deepest fear is not that we are inadequate. Our deepest fear is that we are powerful beyond measure." – Marianne Williamson

I may come across as dark and brooding, but deep down I'm an optimist. I had to be given what I went through. No matter how bad off I was, I tried to imagine a brighter future. Even when I was 80 pounds and could hardly stand on my own, I kept the belief that full recovery from anorexia was possible. Knowing that there were women who had achieved this helped me keep that belief alive. It helped keep me alive, period. The women who had recovered were some of the strongest women I knew. I hardly considered myself among these brave souls. On the contrary, I thought them in a league far beyond my capabilities, yet even today with a body that's somewhat ravaged by years of self-destruction, I have hope.

I have found some odd similarities in the phases of recovery in talking to others who have gone through an eating disorder. The majority of the people who have had anorexia, for example, had a fixation on eating frozen yogurt. It seems a strange irony that with such severe restrictions on food, we would all include frozen yogurt in our limited diets. Of course, not all anorexics consume frozen yogurt, but it's interesting to note that many do. Frozen yogurt can be consumed slowly and is filling and satisfying. In an odd sense, it's the perfect diet food because it's low in fat and can be consumed in small amounts while still providing oral satisfaction and satiety. In addition, a great number of people who were in the very beginning stages of recovery develop a weakness for cereal, especially granola. One woman I know had severe cravings for bagels, but the majority of the individuals I met preferred cereal. In fact, most of us actually binged on it at one time or another. It could be that cereal provides a wide variety of soothing textures and much-needed carbohydrates, but there seems to be an emotional response to cereal as well. It's a food associated with childhood, for example – one that often conjures up images of Saturday mornings watching cartoons on TV. Cereal tends to have crunch appeal too, which is not only satisfying but can also help reduce tension. Unfortunately, the damage to the body that results from anorexia is unpredictable, and each body responds differently to the harsh conditions of starvation. Therefore, no recovery can be a carbon copy of another, and healing becomes a unique experience.

In many ways, anorexia is a blatant example of a

vicious cycle. The more the body is deprived of nutrients, the more it shuts down and the more distorted the person's thinking becomes. The digestive system in particular is affected when one is under extreme stress and starvation conditions. As the body ages, levels of hydrochloric acid and digestive enzymes naturally decrease. This occurs more rapidly under stress. In the case of anorexia, it's almost assured to happen rather quickly. The decrease in natural digestive juices leads to an inability to properly digest and absorb nutrients. This disruption can leave one feeling bloated and full, and can actually further starve the body of essential nutrients. In addition, there are neurons in the gastrointestinal tract that help transmit a wide variety of neurotransmitters, such as serotonin. Serotonin, in addition to having an effect on mood, also affects movement in the intestine. Damage to the neurons in the intestines can be caused by a variety of stressors, including parasites or pinworms, and can lead to a disruption of the transmission of neurotransmitters. It is assumed that improper nutrition can damage all cells in the body, including these neurons, decreasing the transmission of "feel-good" chemicals throughout. So even when normal eating resumes, it's no guarantee that the body will come around and heal itself completely.

When I was in my late thirties, I was diagnosed with anemia, leaky-gut syndrome – a condition that affects the lining of the bowl – and several food allergies. My body is completely wrecked from years of overtraining and starvation. I have had so many stress fractures I have lost count: at least five in my feet, several in my pelvis, one in my heel – the list goes on. I have shortened tendons, stiff muscles, muscle shutdown and chronic back, leg, foot and hip pain. My digestive system is a mess, I fatigue easily, and my immune system is as delicate as a rare orchid in a windstorm. All of this sounds terrible, yet I'm happier now than I have ever been in the past. It may sound impossible to have so many problems and be happy, but considering where I once was, it's true. I can't stress enough that my worst days now are far better than my best days when I was sick. Any pain or trauma in my life now pales in comparison to the darkness of anorexia. No matter how bad things get, I truly believe it will never be as bad as what I went through. I know it's impossible to avoid pain and loss altogether, but I am more capable of moving through the hard times and better able to face uncomfortable feelings now. In addition, I feel that my health is returning. With continued efforts to eat well and manage moderate exercise, it's highly likely that in time, my body will reach equilibrium.

In the meantime, I contemplate how this illness has served me. What was the payoff in staying sick versus getting well? The more I recover, the more responsibility I'm forced to take. As I see it, my anorexia helped me survive. It was a way for me to cope with events I felt were beyond my control. In order for true health to emerge, it's important for me to find new coping mechanisms, ones that will better serve me in this lifetime. I must find the self-esteem and courage to speak out and stand up for myself rather than use harsh self-abusive methods to get messages across.

These days I'm haunted less by calorie-counting and compulsive exercise, and have relaxed the reins a bit. I no longer starve myself, and I don't work out when I'm sick or overly tired. I have also cut back on exercise to a more reasonable amount of time per day. If I look at recovery and illness as a U, where the top of one side represents where I was before the anorexia started and the bottom of the U represents my lowest point, I would say I have climbed up from the bottom of the U, but have not yet reached the top of the opposite side. I can, however, see the top, or at least know that the top does exist. In addition, life has become more enjoyable as I let go of something that no longer serves me.

Most of the girls I know who have suffered through an eating disorder are in a boat similar to mine, somewhere between normal and anorexic. I have heard that most normal people have occasional body-image issues and struggles with food. I had a dream that if I could take a real leap of faith and land in infinite wisdom, I could learn to love my body, my mind and myself. Once, when I was running with a friend, we discussed how powerful the mind is. I told my friend I knew someone who stated that when one puts a heartfelt thought out to the universe, it becomes manifest. We came to the conclusion that if somebody truly believes something, it could and should come true. If this theory is applied to eating habits, it's interesting to look at what our core beliefs around food are, how deserving we feel we are, and what our thought patterns are regarding what we put in our mouths. It's not so much "you are what you eat" but "you are what you think about what you eat." I'm not advocating that everyone go on a chocolate-truffle rampage, or that simply by thinking that consuming all of that chocolate is healthy the body will respond accordingly, but perhaps this theory is not so far-fetched. At least it offers some much-needed relief from the guilt that many of us experience when we don't eat the most balanced of diets.

What I have noticed for myself in the last few years is that while I continue to dance with my illness, we have longer periods apart. At times, I become so immersed in a moment that I forget to be anorexic. This shows me that there is the potential to string more and more of these moments together. Living in the moment is not easy for someone who has spent years planning every meal, every workout and every second of every day, but every time I am able to live in the moment I know I'm doing the right thing for myself.

Oddly enough, I am happier with my body and more accepting of it now than when I was at my sickest. At 80 pounds, I constantly felt fat. Today, I sometimes forget my body. It has taken some time to learn to be kinder to myself, but I have had many people giving me support along the way. I once had to cut somebody out of my life for being too insensitive about my issues. It has taken a long time for me to be able to hear "you look good" or "you look healthy" or "you look great" and not feel fat. However, before I reached this point in the beginning stages of recovery, an acquaintance who had not seen me in several months met me for coffee. He said, "Wow, you look so…" and gestured with his hands as if he were feeling the weight of a large melon. I shook my head and immediately said, "Don't even go there." But he continued. "So meaty!" he concluded, smiling. Rather than throw my glass of water in his face like I wanted, I calmly said, "I can't believe you could say that to someone who had anorexia for nearly 20 years. That was so not the right thing to say." Somehow I was polite as we finished our coffee, but I couldn't let it go. I fretted about my eating for three days and convinced myself I was indeed fat. It saddened me to know that I could give someone this kind of power and not trust myself to even know whether or not I was at a reasonable weight. In the end, I came to the conclusion that my weight was fine for me. The next time I saw this guy, I told him I didn't want any contact with him. It was a hard and somewhat drastic move, yes, but at the time it was what I needed to do. I couldn't risk a slide back into my illness. I wasn't strong enough to be unaffected by comments like this. Eventually, I did forgive him, but at the time I knew it was unhealthy for me to be in his company. He seemed completely unable to understand how his comment had hurt me, and it seemed likely that he would spit out hurtful comments again.

Sometimes, when people ask how I recovered as much as I have, I don't really have an answer. I wish I could tell others who are suffering from this illness that you do x, y and z and then you are well. Unfortunately, anorexia is a very complex illness. I honestly don't think that hospitals, doctors or therapists have all the answers. All these avenues can lead to a greater understanding of the disease, but it's rare that any of them provide the cure. One thing that bothers me the most about a hospital setting is it doesn't in any way prepare the individual to deal with life outside. Relapses in anorexia are more common than not. However, those who want to get well are far less likely to relapse. One has to want to get well and want it extremely badly before any change is likely to hold. Finding the courage to even express the desire to get well can be overwhelming from the perspective of an anorexic who feels helplessly trapped. Recognizing that the path to recovery is not easy, but can lead to a much better life, eases the tension of taking that first step, be it calling a counselor, admitting to a loved one or contacting a treatment center.

I wish I had the backbone and merit to wear one of those, "I Beat Anorexia" T-shirts with conviction. However, I feel that I allow my illness to lurk around in the shadows too much for me to believe in my heart that I am completely recovered. Learning to trust innate wisdom is the ultimate goal of anyone struggling to be healthy. A forgiving nature toward the self is essential for recovery. When first learning to eat better and let go of the harsh thinking patters of anorexia, I often had to ask myself if I would treat someone else this way. If the answer was no, I knew I was being too strict with myself. Strangely, it is often easier to treat others well. Treating myself with that same compassion and understanding has been difficult. Finding the strength to continue to make healthier choices can sometimes be fatiguing, but it has definitely made me a stronger, more sympathetic person. Maybe one day I will be proud enough to sport a t-shirt that lets people know I conquered my illness. Until then, I'm content to just be alive, all things considered.

I know full recovery is possible. I have seen it. There are women out there who lead full lives, no longer haunted by the anorexia demons that once ruled their existence. But the road to recovery is not easy. If I had known how hard it would be, I might not have made the essential first leap of faith that I did. On the other hand, now that I'm in a much better place, there's no way I would ever, ever go back.

* * *

Chapter 35 – A Holistic Approach

"Healing takes courage, and we all have courage, even if we have to dig a little to find it." – Tori Amos

When things were terrible with my illness, and I was wading through the muck and the mire, I searched for the proverbial magic pill that would cure me. Of course, there was none to be found, but it didn't stop me from wanting to find something that would cure me from this illness that had me in its icy grip. If someone had told me that rubbing a garlic clove on my nose would fix me, I probably would have tried it. I was desperate. While I didn't find true magic, I did find many alternative approaches to healing that captured my interest and seemed to work for many people. If these modalities of healing didn't help me directly, the process of trying something new taught me to keep searching for what would work for me. I believe that everyone is capable of finding the right combination of remedies, therapies and inner peace that will lead to a better and happier life.

When one takes a look at less traditional forms of healing, it's important to note that the focus is not on the symptom itself but more on the energetic balance of the being in general. Symptoms provide a clue as to what is going on deeper in the body or mind. According to Chardin Bersto, M.A., in the case of, for example, five-element healing,"we're looking at a new way of coming to the human form from an energetic perspective as opposed to physical." His somatics method "integrates the contemporary thinking of Quantum and Unified Field Theories with spirituality. Thus you will learn to see yourself and others as having many choices within a wide field of possibilities." His work frees the individual from the physical manifestations of old thoughts and limiting beliefs by balancing the five elements: earth, water, metal, fire and wood.

The foundation of the work is the pulse. According to Daniel Redwood, DC, acupuncturists take a similar approach and look at the whole person. A treatment plan is devised on an individual basis, taking into account not only overt symptoms, but also the patient's constitutional makeup and the factors that weaken and strengthen them. Diagnosis includes a subtle reading of the wrist pulses, which indicate the flow or blockage of qi (the Chinese word meaning "vital energy") that flows through the body's acupuncture meridians, or pathways.

The way Chardin looks at something like illness or injury is very different from the way a physical therapist or a standard medical doctor does. The latter focus on the symptoms only and treatment of those symptoms. Chardin points out, "Particular restrictions occur in our body as the result of how we come in contact with the world. In the process of a person's life, in osteopathy one may refer to the 'key lesion' or original injury that can go back as far as in utero. The work that I do treats the span of the person's life." He adds that "Stress translates into mal adaptation of an organ or meridian. Even stress from the mother can translate to trauma to the fetus." In general, one should be able to heal readily from either physical or emotional trauma, but if there are blockages, that healing may be diminished. Stressors that cause blockages can be as big as a car accident or as subtle as a child getting his feelings hurt.

Though there are now medications available that diminish the effect of post-traumatic stress, Chardin states, "In Chinese medicine, pharmaceuticals create deficiencies in the body. Medications tend to weaken other parts of the body. In terms of rehabilitation of the being, it doesn't work. Carl Jung always felt that tension is the seed of change, so to get rid of tension doesn't serve the person's soul."

With anorexia, instead of seeing a treatment plan that is the same for all patients, Chardin cautions: "Anorexia is a system-dynamic challenge. Some perception occurred in the course of the person's life that led them into using behaviors around their eating, and also the idea of self-concept plays into this. If you take one hundred people with anorexia, you will get a different reading on each one. The key lesion becomes the center of a particular tensional constellation in the body, because we're dealing with a body that stands in gravity. If you have a weakness in one part of the body, another has to take over and a pattern develops." The result is pain or tension in that part of the body, which can be traced back to and is also a symptom of the key lesion.

The development of self is a core issue in healing. Chardin explains, "As children we are innocent. Children have an energetic relationship to the world that is completely permeable. They experience the world in an energetic manner more than adults. They can pick up on things that are happening in the family system. When it comes to healing, the family can actually be seen as an entire working system." Chardin asks, "What is that symptom or, if you look at the family as an entire system, what is the individual with the illness trying to accomplish within the whole system?"

Chardin's work includes "balancing of the pulses in order to repolarize the spaces in the body that have been held in tension. A pulse is in direct contact with the connective tissue matrix field and tells me by its weakness or strength or overabundance where the problems in the body live." It is a very subtle practice in which twenty-nine different qualities of the pulse are detected. It is known to be very similar to the Ayurvedic practice of pulse-reading.

When looking at diet and nutrition, Chardin continues to stick to the five elements and balancing these elements with appropriate foods that correlate to each. In this way, food is considered energetically, not nutritionally. The focus is on how food can help balance any imbalance in the body through color, flavor and even temperature. If your attitude about eating is tied up in a past event and that behavior no longer serves you, you must consider what you can choose differently that will nurture who you are.

As we grow and develop, stages of our lives correlate with the different elements as well. You may notice that many people approaching their forties and fifties become more at ease with themselves. According to Chinese medicine, this stage of life correlates to the earth element, settling in to who you are.

Similar to the ancient Chinese method of healing with the five elements is the Shamanic approach to healing. According to Heather Clewett-Jachowski, founder of Inkavisions in Sedona, Arizona: "In the Inka tradition, we are in a sacred relationship with the wisdom of Ayni. Ayni means balance. As caretakers of the Earth, Shamans must walk the path of Ayni. Only this commitment will allow the Shaman to assist others in bringing their lives into balance.

"Shamans will not collude with you about the disorder that is eating you, or the truck that hit you on the way to work, or the jaguar that ate you at the watering hole. Regardless of the story, Shamans will ask you, how is it that your life is out of balance – out of Ayni – and how can I help?

"In these interesting times, we each have chosen a difficult birthing process for our souls' evolution. The secret that has been kept from us, and that we have agreed to keep even from ourselves, is that we are Spiritual beings. We always have been; we always will be; it has always been this way. This creates the knowing that we are responsible for the human experiences we each choose along our paths. As we remember that we are Spiritual beings choosing human experiences, we become the wisdom-keepers we've been waiting for. As we bring our lives individually and collectively into balance – into Ayni – we dream awake a healed world into being."

No matter what approach one takes to getting well, it's crucial to view the individual as more than her illness or injury. A more holistic view is essential, especially with anorexia, which includes obvious physical as well as emotional issues. In nearly all modalities of treatment, healing occurs by bringing that which is out of balance back into balance. What's important to know is that the body in balance can heal itself.

* * *

Chapter 36 – How Lucky I Am

"I like living. I have sometimes been wildly, despairingly, acutely miserable, racked with sorrow, but through it all I still know that just to be alive is a grand thing." – Agatha Christie

The study of eating disorders is a relatively new

field, so there are varying statistics on recovery rates. There is a general consensus that left untreated, 20 percent of those with an eating disorder will die from it. It has been suggested that only 20 to 25 percent fully recover, with somewhere between 20 to 30 percent left to continue to struggle with eating issues. Another 10 to 20 percent do not improve, even with treatment, and live marginal lives consumed with daily struggles around food, body image and weight.

As with any addiction, the first step in recovery is to admit that there is a problem. Often, family members become so tired from trying to save the affected individual that they must at some point retreat and protect themselves. This does not mean family members no longer love or support the individual, only that they have come to the conclusion that anyone with anorexia has to want to get well for himself or herself before help can be provided. Recovery takes a long-term commitment; some promise that no matter how bad things get, health is the ultimate goal. It is impossible for someone on the outside to force recovery. However, because anorexia is a life-threatening illness, it is essential to provide options for anyone suffering from this disorder. Interventions and suggestions should not be discounted. It's impossible to know whether taking action or giving advice will resonate with an anorexic, but it's important to keep trying. It was Dick Van Dyke who once said that with his alcoholism, 100 people gave him the same piece of advice, but he wasn't ready to hear it until the 101st person said it. In other words, timing is everything when it comes to recovery, just as it was for me when my sister finally told me how my eating disorder had affected her and that I needed to take responsibility for my own recovery. I wasn't ready to change before that. In severe cases of anorexia, a hospital setting may be most appropriate, simply so that the patient can be carefully watched on a 24-hour-a-day basis.

Once the decision to get well has been made, there are many physical and emotional hurdles to clear. Anti-depressants, either synthetic or all-natural (e.g., SAM-e, TravaCor, or St John's wort) can take the edge off the depression and anxiety that often accompany an eating disorder. Unfortunately, there are many physical symptoms with which to contend once regular eating is resumed. Digestive enzymes, pancreatin and hydrochloric acid can ease bloating, gas, and that uncomfortable full feeling while helping the body absorb more nutrients. With severe malnourishment, intravenous vitamin drips can be most beneficial. A good multivitamin and mineral tablet – especially one that contains an adequate amount of zinc, a mineral that has been shown to improve the symptoms of anorexia – is crucial when adequate daily nutrients are missing from the diet. Ultimately the body is resilient and is able to repair itself when given the chance. Healing is possible. With proper nutrients and an improved mental outlook, the healing process can occur more quickly.

Lorraine Moller and Colleen Cannon, two former world-class athletes, have an approach to eating and health that goes beyond using food merely as fuel. Their thoughts on the topic are truly inspirational.

Lorraine was able to convey what I consider to be crucial to recovery: the evolution of the self. She says, "The truth of who you are is wonderful. It seems we are often struggling to make our inner reality match our outer world. Everywhere we're caught up on this idea that we're not okay."

I sat for a moment and thought how often my fear and lack of self respect allowed me to be taken advantage of by others. In addition, I thought about how undeserving of praise, money, and of course food I often felt. My inner reality of being not okay enough to deserve the good in life was certainly being reflected in my posture, look and overall physique. Lorraine goes into detail about this:

> We tend to limit ourselves in the world by labeling ourselves, and freedom comes only when we move away from these labels. . In discovering the core of who we are, not defined by outer appearance, others or outdated internal belief systems, we open up to a world of possibilities. The more emotionally invested we are in our weight, the more we move away from performance. You have to ask yourself, "how far will I go to

reach my goal?" If you are unable to move forward and are stuck in your identity, it can be miserable, but this is a sign that resolution is needed. It's time to integrate a larger perspective and fulfill your potential as a creative loving being. Whenever we come up against something that's not working in our lives, we need to figure out in which way we're not loving ourselves. We need to be continually reinventing ourselves and move from one experience to the next. If everything in life is suggesting a change, and, instead, stagnation is achieved, it can lead to heartache, sorrow and pain.

In terms of my own performance, it did suffer. Had I not been so caught up in being thin, it's possible I could have focused more on how to improve my running. It's as if I was too thin to consistently do well and too hungry to focus on the things that mattered, yet too afraid to change. I had competing goals, and being thin eventually won over being an outstanding athlete. I often wonder how much I used my eating disorder as an excuse to not do well. It was obvious that I was too weak to run well in the long term, but somehow it was important to me at the time to know that I was thin, as if that's any kind of measure of success. It's not. If anything, it showed how out of balance my life had become. My focus of doing something exceptionally well had shifted to a focus on weight. If I had allowed myself to eat outside the strict rules I had set for myself, there's a good chance that my running career would have been much longer and might have flourished rather than fizzled.

When it comes to therapy, Lorraine suggests that this can be helpful, but only in that therapy and other modalities of healing lead to a better understanding of the self. What's more important to recognize is how self-imposed limitations are keeping the spirit from full expression:

The spirit keeps wanting expression.
As we learn and grow, our world needs
to expand accordingly to encompass
more, and it should be more wonderful.
It's the same with training. If you train
right, you should be getting better and
faster and having more fun. The body is a
vehicle for the spirit's expression. [If spirit
isn't a term that resonates, one can think
of it simply as moving on when it's time,
regardless of any spiritual beliefs] We
don't want to get stuck in one archetype.
We want to be able to express ourselves
in many ways throughout life.

As Jackson Pollock once said, "It doesn't make much difference how the paint is put on as long as something is being said. Technique is just a means of arriving at a statement." For those of us who can no longer run to make a statement, we must find other means of expression.

Before my interview with Lorraine came to a close, she mentioned some ideas to help with the recovery process. The concept is based on how core beliefs can be changed:

Thoughts always follow beliefs, but you always have your creative genius which comes in like divine inspiration and can put in a crack in your belief system. This is where you have the first step. Something that changes your thoughts and makes you realize that maybe there is another way. We have thoughts, which is basically an internal process, and words that are an expression following thoughts. Words are one step farther into reality than thoughts. Then we have action based on these thoughts that is actually putting ourselves out into the world, going even farther into reality, so if our actions are based on thoughts and ultimately on our beliefs, we can work backward by deliberately using action to send the feedback system a new message. This action, even if it's scary, will reinforce a new belief. Words can be used as well to create a new pathway to a new belief

system. A good exercise is to look in the
mirror and see the beauty in you. Say out
loud 'I look beautiful' even if thoughts
come up that are contrary. Eventually the
statement can become part of a new
reality for you.

Having tried this exercise, I can say that it's not
one that's as easy as it sounds. All the years of telling
myself I was ugly got in the way of seeing any of the
beauty in me.

I asked Lorraine why it's so common for us to
put limitations on ourselves. Her feelings:

Limitations are part of the soul's
journey. They can be taught by parents or
the people around us or they can be self
imposed, but since we are in this reality to
learn about love, we can't learn about
love without first knowing what love isn't.
We need to move away from the model
of the body as a machine and look at it
more as an energetic unit. As we move
toward this model, it's important to also
look at food not as compartments of
calories, fat and carbohydrates and
instead look at food as something that
nourishes us. Ask what the life force
behind the food is. For example, a piece
of cake baked by a loving grandmother

will have a whole different energetic feel to it than a piece of cake that has been sitting on the shelf that's filled with preservatives and artificial ingredients. The one baked by the loving grandmother is sure to have a much higher life energy around it. If I look at beliefs around food, my body will get a very different message based on what I put in my mouth than the message sent when someone else eats the same thing. It's all how we view it and our beliefs around it."

* * *

Chapter 37 – Conclusion

"The universe never says no to your thought about yourself. It only grows it." – Neale Donald Walsch

My first impression of Colleen Cannon when I met her years ago was "this woman is strong." She radiated an aura of confidence and self-acceptance, and it was no surprise to find out she was a world-class triathlete. As an athlete, Colleen was lucky to have avoided an eating disorder. Years later, when

I met her for an interview to discuss exactly how she achieved this, she still radiated the confidence of a world-class athlete.

"Through my career I learned that there's no good or bad way to eat. I came from a sprinter's background and had a brother on the football team, so bigger wasn't necessarily a bad thing." She says. "On the track, bigger meant stronger and we could go faster. We ate fried chicken after races and didn't think twice about it." Colleen's coaches felt otherwise and pressured her to lose weight. At one point her track coach even cut her off from the Haagen Dazs store, warning the staff there not to serve his athlete. Although Colleen was far from fat, she was bigger than the average runner, yet she was able to hold the school record for the 1500-meter run in college, a standard that would last for nearly 20 years. "I wasn't going to not eat, so I just ate the ice cream or whatever I wanted anyway and ran well despite what my coaches told me," she says.

Like Lorraine Moller, Colleen looks at food not just as an energy source for the physical body but as something that connects us to the universe:

> The way people eat has a lot to do with beliefs. Food is condensed God juice. I say God not in the religious sense, but however you want to interpret it. Food connects us to the divine. The sun grows the plants that feed the cows. It

even helps grow the people who make the Twinkies!

For me, I have learned to go by how I feel. I learned a lot from Dr. Phil Maffetone, who educated me on the benefits of including fats in the diet. As I ate more of what my body needed and craved, I felt better and more connected, centered. Athletes are more prone to try various fad diets to see what will make them perform best, but it's really more about being present when you eat.

When power bars first came out, a few of us were involved in an experiment where we ate a certain ratio of fats, carbohydrates and proteins and these power bars. After the third day, I felt flat and almost depressed. It was no fun. After eating the same bars for three days, it seemed like the bars had no life force in them. It felt good to return to regular eating again after the study.

Colleen mentioned that merely holding the food in a sacred place or blessing the food can help get that connection to the divine or to the higher self. If we are calm and fully present when we eat, the food is more likely to nourish us in the ways we want. "I ran a race once with another triathlete, and at a pre-race dinner, we were shocked to see all these skinny competitors eating apple wedges," she recalls. "The two of us had big bowls of pasta in front of us, and for a moment I questioned whether I should be eating it. Then I said to my pasta, 'Pasta, you're gonna make me run so fast tomorrow,' and I did!"

After a successful career as a professional triathlete, Colleen founded a camp called Women's Quest, where women can learn to get in touch with their inner desires. Training techniques, mind-body-spirit connection exercises and other activities are provided to help individuals discover more about themselves. Colleen says, "The camp is a safe environment for people to find the heart's desire and any obstacles in the way of achieving that heart's desire. It seems like food always comes up as an issue for women, so it's good that the people who run the camps are all different sizes and shapes. That way it shows that self acceptance doesn't have to be based on a certain body type. We also look at all the ways to nourish the self, not just through food."

I may not be the epitome of health, but I'm better than when I was anorexic. I keep searching and working to find answers that will lead to my body healing more fully and allow me to live a more comfortable life. Despite the long-term consequences my body has suffered as a result of being anorexic, I have once again found passion. I am able to throw myself into my writing, into my work and into just being human. I have wonderful relationships with the people around me. I am fully supported and able to set my illness aside and actually live in the world again. Each day I face the choice of whether to give in to old patters or try something new. The more I can trust the universe and allow for change, the more at ease I can become in my own body and my own ability to read it.

I still run. I'm no longer training on empty. Setting records and winning races are no longer on my mind, though I remember those days well. I run because my body, even with all that I put it through, has allowed me to return to a sport that I love. With countless injuries, many surgeries and years of illness behind me, I now run with the freedom of someone who has returned from the edge. Days off are not as much of a struggle as they once were, and I'm to the point where I can enjoy rest. The overly critical part of my brain is not as active, and this allows me to be kinder to myself. Anorexia once enveloped my mind. Food, my weight and running were all I thought about. Eventually, these things drifted to the background, but I was still unduly aware. Now my mind is less encumbered with these thoughts than it ever has been. It was a combination of time and work that got me to this place. I had to rediscover who I was and be okay with simply being me.

Surviving something like an eating disorder naturally brings up big questions such as "why am I here?" or "who am I?" At times I am still searching for answers to questions about life. Coming so close to dying and then recovering to experience life in a new way is something I may never understand. My hope is that I can provide some inspiration to others and maybe even prevent people from having to go through what I did. I believe that as with any illness, the sooner the problem is dealt with, the better the chances of a full recovery. With so many people inflicted with some sort of eating disorder, it's essential for those of us who have survived to come forward, whether we still have days we struggle with it or not. I sincerely believe that the more an example of good health is held up and admired, the more others will follow suit and toss out the disturbing notion that a sickly anorexic model is to be adored. If I look to those who have truly been an inspiration to me, I would have to admit that their inspiration had nothing to do with their body size or what they ate. No, heroes and heroines are not made by a certain diet; they are made by having a compassionate, loving nature and a strong confident character. Through all my struggles with food, weight and body image, I keep the concept of these heroes in my mind and strive every day to become more like one of these brave souls.

Organizations:
ANAD national Association of Anorexia Nervosa and Associated Disorders; (847) 831-3438, http://www.anad.org.
National Anorexia & Bulimia Association (NABA); (402) 371-0722;

http://www.nabassociation.org.
Eating-Disorder.com; (866)-575-8179.
Connects people with the appropriate treatment centers.

Books:
Geneen Roth:
How to Break Free from Compulsive Eating
Feeding the Hungry Heart
When Food is Love
Peggy Claude-Pierre:
The Secret Language of Eating Disorders
Linda Rector Page, N.D., Ph.D.
Healthy Healing

Web sites:
http://www.something-fishy.org/
http://www.edreferral.com/
http://mentalhelp.net/poc/center_index.php?id=46
www.anred.com

* * *

When I initially began this book, I wanted to provide inspiration to others and show that eating disorders can be overcome. During my illness, I looked not only to those who had recovered, but to those who had avoided an eating disorder altogether, for these people showed great courage and strength in allowing their true potential to emerge under the many pressures that this society inflicts. A special thanks to some of the amazing people who have encouraged and inspired me to be well, and for their take on anorexia and its cure:

Heather Clewett-Jacowski
Founder of Inkavisions in Sedona, Arizona (www.inkavisions.com), Heather was trained by Dr. Alberto Villoldo, founder of The Four Winds Society and author of *Shaman, Healer, Sage.* She has also traveled with and been trained by the Q'ero high in the Peruvian Andes. The Q'ero are the last remaining Inka Shaman elders skilled in the ancient healing methods of the Inka and pre-Inka. Their techniques involve working on illness and emotional wounds before any symptoms manifest in the physical body.

Bobby McGee
Bobby McGee is a full-time endurance coach who owns Bobby McGee Endurance Sports, a Colorado-based sports company. He has coached numerous Olympians in distance running and triathlon. He works with both elite athletes and the average weekend warrior. He is also involved with coaching education, lectures, has written numerous articles and has published numerous books, including *Magical Running; A Unique Path to Running Fulfillment,* a book that deals with the mental aspects of running; and *Running Sports Essentials,* a manual that covers supplementary exercises for runners. He can be

reached through his Web site, www.BobbyMcGee.com.

Diane Israel, M.A.
Diane was a very successful professional triathlete and runner. She won many triathlon races around the world, including the bronze medal at the Macabea Games, and is best known for being the 1984 Colorado mountain-running champion. After retiring from professional competition, she pursued her academic goals to become a psychotherapist. She produced the film *Beauty Mark* (http://www.beautymarkmovie.com/), which addresses body image and the disconnect between mind and body. Diane is on the faculty at Naropa University, teaching graduate courses in transpersonal psychology. She is also the owner of Gyrotonic® Boulder, and guides people in physical, mental, and spiritual integration. She provides amazingly strong support and camaraderie for participants in body image, nutrition and rekindling life's passions and direction. Most of all, Diane is a kindred spirit on the path of whole-life health and balance.

Lorraine Moller
Lorraine is a four-time Olympian, a three-time world champion, an Olympic bronze medalist, and the winner of sixteen major international marathons, including the Boston marathon. She holds the distinction of being the only woman to have run each of the first four Olympic women's marathons. Her

twenty-eight years as an international athlete are unprecedented in distance running, and she credits her success to her unique and creative approach to competition, training, and learning to play with space and time. In 1993, Lorraine was awarded an MBE (Member of the British Empire) by Her Majesty, Queen Elizabeth II. She captured her amazingly full life in her 2007 autobiography, *On the Wings of Mercury.*

Along with her running achievements, Lorraine was a forerunner for equality in women's athletics, and an activist for professionalism in distance running. Since retiring from competitive sport in 1996, this long-time Boulder resident has continued her travels as the vice president of Hearts of Gold, a charitable organization that raises money through running events in Japan, Cambodia and Mongolia. On the home front, Lorraine coaches Olympic hopefuls, teaches remote viewing, writes for various fitness publications, and does the occasional sports television commentary. Forever a student of the spirit-mind-body connection, Lorraine is a keen student of alchemy and mythology.

Colleen Cannon

Colleen founded Women's Quest (http://www.womensquest.com) after a highly successful career as a professional triathlete. In her racing days, she was the World Triathlon Champion in 1984, and National Triathlon Champion in 1988 and

1990. She also was a multiple U.S. National Team member. Her passions, besides chocolate and being in nature, are liberating and empowering women through movement and balance, and targeting their true hearts' desire. Colleen continues to evolve adventures for Women's Quest, delighting in ways to enchant women with the experiences that coax happiness grown from joyful physical experiences.

Kevin Beck

Kevin Beck is a senior writer for *Running Times* Magazine, the editor of the training book *Run Strong*, and the author of a wide variety of health- and fitness-related articles. Active in the running community for over a quarter of a century, he has staged exercise clinics for the Boy Scouts of America, coached high-school cross-country and track teams, and given pre-race marathon talks. He also coaches a cadre of marathoners, several of whom have reached the U.S. Olympic Trials standard. With a best time of 2 hours, 24 minutes himself, he was one of the top Americans at the 2001 Boston Marathon. In 2004, Kevin placed second in the USATF 50K National Road Championship. Also a freelance editor, Kevin is a passionate wordsmith and is in the process of writing a novel. For more information, visit him online at http://www.kemibe.com

Chardin Bersto, M.A.

Chardin has an M.A. in Psychology from Sonoma

State University and a B.A. from CSU-Chico, with a double major in Psychology and Religious Studies and an emphasis in Eastern Religions. He has practiced Somatics since 1979, and has studied Chinese Medicine, Acupressure, Shiatsu, Applied Kinesiology, Postural Integration, Rolfing, Polarity Therapy, Cranio-Sacral and Visceral Manipulation, Mayan Organ Manipulation, Chi Ni San (an organ Manipulation style from Chinese Medicine), and Yoga, since 1974. He has been teaching for 10 years. A student of human anatomy since childhood, Chardin studied nursing and was a Physician's Assistant in the Navy.

Julie Threlkeld
Julie Threlkeld is a freelance writer, editor and editorial content strategist. She is also a late blooming road racer and an avid follower of the sport's past and present. She is honored to have been able to make a modest contribution to the editing of this memoir. She blogs at www.raceslikeagirl.com.

Jennifer St. Germain-Cole
Jennifer offers a wide variety of services for writers, including editing, manuscript restructuring and proofreading. Her Web site, Writer's Plus, is at http://writersplus.books.officelive.com/default.aspx.

Additional Acknowledgements:

Special thanks to Janine, Bobby, my family, Annie, Heather, Diane, Lorraine, Dave, Julie, Kevin, Jennifer, Colleen, Nathan, Debbie, Myra, Sharon, Patty, Lori, Laura, Katie, Peg, Janet, James, Geoff, Rocky, Joan, Liza, Britta, Marci, Trystin, Tracy, Clint, Le'a, Sara, Sarah S., Sarah G., Kate, Katrina, Josh, David and Judy, Mark, Brian, Katie, Dr Stanly, Dr Terry, Dr Shackleton, Chardin, Eric, Dr. Robert Jelinek, Scott, my friends, fellow pirates, other doctors, and anyone else out there struggling in this world.

# # #

Made in the USA
San Bernardino, CA
29 January 2016